BECOMING THE Woman GOD INTENDED ME TO BE

Dr. Tacoma R. Anderson

website: www.tacomaanderson.com

Library of Congress Control Number: 2020900428
ISBN 978-1-955156-09-7 (paperback)
ISBN 978-1-955156-10-3 (digital)

Copyright © 2021 by Dr. Tacoma R. Anderson

All rights reserved. No part of this publication may be reproduced, distributed, or transmitted in any form or by any means, including photocopying, recording, or other electronic or mechanical methods without the prior written permission of the publisher. For permission requests, solicit the publisher via the address below.

Cover photo by Mr Joseph Wright
Vividviewphotos@gmail.com

Scripture quotations marked KJV are from the Holy Bible, King James Version (Authorized Version). First published in 1611. Quoted from the KJV Classic Reference Bible, Copyright © 1983 by The Zondervan Corporation.

Rushmore Press LLC
1 800 460 9188
www.rushmorepress.com

Printed in the United States of America

First and Foremost, I give honor to Jesus Christ, my Lord, Savior, King, lover of my soul and head of my life. I wrote this book for the distinct purpose of providing some encouragement to others in the mist of their struggles. The storm is just a process; though it may seem never ending it is truly full of Character-building moments! This is not the time to lose faith in God but to hold stronger to it, God has a plan for your life Jeremiah 29:11, it is worth the struggle.

This book is dedicated to all who are in the Ministry, who have a desire to know God intimately and those who are trusting God to bring them through by taking Him at His word. I also Dedicate it to those who have influenced me the most in life, My Dad, may he rest in Peace, my Son Ahmad, my godson, my sons godfather Arnold Arrington, my Aunts and Uncles, my military big brothers and sisters, my battle buddies from Somalia, my hometown friends and family and those who have sown into my spiritual Journey -My spiritual mentors.

I pray that this book will let you know your story is just as important to someone as the air we breathe for the story (testimony) is an encouragement or a map to someone who is trying to get to know God as you do and remember you may be the only God this person ever sees. I pray that you are blessed, healed and will be delivered from all forms of bondage especially as you travel on the road to becoming who God has also intended you to be. I pray that as you read these steps to Becoming the Woman God Intended Me to Be you too will be encouraged to press toward the mark of the prize of the high calling of God in Christ Jesus according to Philippians 3:14.

Foreword

When Tacoma Anderson told me she was writing another book I was very excited for her. I have found in knowing her she puts her heart into each book that she publishes. "Becoming The Woman God Intended Me to Be" is such a phenomenal read. As Tacoma's leader I would even say she shows out a bit on writing. She is an author that gives the transparency of what most author do not share in their writings. This book gives way to the fulfillment of the woman from the little girl in them to who God has called them to be. I am impressed with the steps to becoming the woman we need to be in God's image. Tacoma gives precise scriptures to help any woman know the divine purpose of their life when it comes to God. She also encourages us as woman to not count yourself out and rely on God to bring you through and not a man. I love it when she expressed herself as a woman who made mistakes and thought she had found the right man but had not. Although there were times she was hurt to the core God brought her through all that she has been through.

Amazing through ever bruise of life I am encourage to know through the writings of this book that as a woman I have hope in knowing God helps me to become who I am to be. The uncommon way of God that Tacoma expresses in Chapter 22 gives every woman the ability to strive for greater purpose in life. Tacoma Anderson love that it is given in this wonderful success of authorship is truly an open door to most woman that choose to walk in the call that God has called them to in the hour we are in. I am honored to have read and foreward this masterpiece of art. Truly this will make a difference for all woman that will be partakers of it.

Dr. Shonda Kirk

Giving, and touching other's lives and expanding the circle of her love, care, concern and compassion not only to include others but for sake of and on the behalf of others, being authentic, and always being open to giving, receiving and always available to help others is not just some fairy tale, it is an accurate description of some of the most incredible and amazing people I have encountered in my life from all over the world and from different fields; this epitomizes who Dr. Tacoma Anderson is.

This book captures the core values and shows that it is more than a fable, a parable, a fantasy, or a dream. It is real that a person can rise up out of and from the ruins of their shattered life and arrive at "Becoming". Not only is what she shares in this book is real, but it is a path that others can follow in their daily lives as well and arrive at "Becoming" just as she did.

From the first day Dr. Anderson and I met sometime ago we both knew not only did we share the same creative abilities but we had a divine connection in that we both share and write from "our life is an open book" place and point within us. We both share a love for God and a love for those who don't know how to love God, how to love themselves and they don't know how to reach and find the God that is not hidden nor is He mysterious. Dr. Anderson and I are divinely connected and she is open and honest and is sincere and she want to reach and help those who was and is like the person she once was.

She is not churchy nor is she religious but she is real and she write and share from that real place within her. People today want to believe, think and feel that living without a focus on others is not something that has value and is meaningful, but that isn't what Dr. Andersons life and her the writing of "Becoming" is all about. Living with a focus on helping and reaching others isn't just a nice goal for Dr. Anderson but she has made it a way of life that for her has led to a life that is full, rich and fulfilling.

Our life travels and journeys and the paths we had to take may have been different but the things we have been through are identical in that we both had to "go through" what we went through and we both had to learn how to "get through" in order for us to step into our metamorphosis of becoming. What she and I went through may appear to be different but it was "yet the same". She is a woman and a human being of impeccable and unquestionable character and she is a real true role model for those who are search of becoming.

Dr. Anderson clearly depicts and describes the path and her journey into "becoming". It is a path and a journey I know all to well. In my own personal life I learned to "be" the person I always was and I knew all to well how to "end up being" the person I had always been but I struggled and strained to find my way into "becoming" the person God created me to be and into the person I knew I was capable of standing strong and relentless in. I know all to well what it means to live a hindered life, a suicidal life, to be in a holding pattern, seeking validation, looking for love in all of the wrong places and people.

I know firsthand what it means to have people write you off, count you out, what it means to lose hope, and what it really and truly mean to only be holding on to just a glimmer of hope and to not have a not to strong faith and to not feel good enough and what it means to have a tainted and twisted thinking. I have been there! In this book you will discover the secret of God's way of reaching into the ruins of a person's life and resurrecting them into "becoming" not just the woman, but the person, and the human being they were created to be, "become" and end up being.

You will learn about the power of choice and how it can bless you and your life or how it can help or severally hinder, hurt and handicap you and your life. You will learn about generational curses and about desires, and how and why certain things can and will influence us, and about wanting to change and not really knowing how. You will learn how to come to the place of point of completely yielding, submitting and surrendering to your true identification of who you are in God, a woman of faith and a prayer warrior.

You will find out that while she was and you are running from her destiny, she gained the character she needed so she and "you as well" can and will be able and empowered to walk deeper within your destiny. You will also learn how to take hold of your identity that is declared in the word of God, and how to obtain a deeper and clearer understanding of your purpose for Gods kingdom and to his glory and so much, much more.

"Becoming" is an exemplary, honest and an exceptional work in that Dr. Anderson is not afraid to be transparent in allowing you to take a look into her own personal journey into "becoming" as she allows the you the reader to read from the pages of her own life and from the pages of her own personal and private hurt, pain and brokenness. Something that is very rare in today's world because most are so image conscious. You will be tremendously blessed and transformed through what Dr. Anderson opens up the book of her life and share from the pages of her life. Its' not a process, it's not a procedure nor is it a principle nor a formula but it's a journey you will have to take into "Becoming".

Humbly submitted,

Author Prophet Anthony McMaryion
Lodebar Ministries/The Healing Center for Relationships

It's time for you to see yourself as the Amazing Woman God Created You to Be

How often have you fallen short of excellence's and let the frustration you felt make you think you're were inadequate or just not good enough? How many times have you compared yourself with other Women and felt badly about yourself based on what other people wanted you to be? You know in your heart God has more for you. You can feel it and you're ready to step into that place of peace.

Have there been times you knowingly compared your life. your job, your home even your spouse to someone else? Before you were born God, planned your life by design? If you answered yes to any of the above scenario's Dr. Tacoma Anderson shares, biblical truths in her insightful; book that will help you see yourself through the eyes of God.

She's shares her heart so beautifully and openly deeply baring her soul using each decade of her life peppered with personal stories about her hurt, disappointment and painful life lessons along with practical advice, and ways to move your life forward. Dr. Tacoma Anderson addresses the challenges and issues she faced while growing-in the Women God called her to be.

What you glean from her writing is pure honest, transparency, vulnerability, inner strength, fortitude and eventually joy. She's leave's her past behind while redesigning her life to reflect all that she learned through Education, Motherhood, Stellar Military Career, World travels, studying and meditating on the word of God. She has served, worshipped and paying a very dear price allowing God to mold shape her so that she could offer hope to all who read her life's roadmap touching the world along the way "Become The Women God Intended Her To Be.

Bridgette Lewis Author, Mentor, Speaker and Coach

BECOMING THE WOMAN OF GOD INTENDED ME TO BE

My dearest Tacoma, congratulation on another spiritual and heartfelt book, "Becoming The Woman God Intended Me to Be. As your former combat Medical Hospital Commander while deployed to Somalia, I was personally touched by your love, compassion and spiritual comfort you offered and provided to our many wounded service men and women. In your previous book, "The Deepest Part of Me" you somewhat outlined this compassion in your poems "Heart of a Soldier and "A Soldier Thoughts".

Your current book is a blessing to read and I believe that it will encourage all of us to truly trust in God and to reach our destiny. Reading your book "Becoming the Women of GOD Intended Me to Be" is powerful, beautiful, spiritual, uplifting and a motivating book. THANKS so much my gifted one. **YOU ARE THE WOMAN GOD INTENDED YOU TO BE....**

Artie L. Shelton, MD. Colonel (ret) U.S. Army

Preface

There will come a time in your single life if it is not this moment that you have an understanding that you are set aside for God's Glory. This will not always resonate in your mind especially when you have a desire to have a relationship with someone.

I realized that during periods of my young adult life, especially in high school, I didn't get asked out on dates. It was exceptionally hard for me and had an impact on how I began to see myself as a woman. When I was younger many people would tell me that I was beautiful, (outer) and that I could have any man I wanted. That was a straight lie!!!

I learned the hard way as time passed that the other person must desire to invest in you the same as you desire to invest your time, energy and emotions into them. I had to learn to value the guys who didn't want to date me because they were looking for more than what I was willing to give physically. I learned to respect the guys who were honest enough to say things like "you are not the dating type; you are the marrying type". I didn't see the value then but I truly appreciate those guys who had the heart to be honest about where they were in life and where I didn't fit into their life.

I learned to value the way that my dad always raised my sisters and I to conduct ourselves as ladies. That even when I was trying to fit in with the crowd, I stood out because my character and conduct spoke volumes to those who had public view of my life.

Even when I went to the military straight from High school, God placed special people in my life to keep me accountable to the way

I was raised. They were the gate keepers, who keep the hawks and hounds at bay as I tried to discover being an adult on my own.

I had to learn fast and the hard way about making myself to assessable to men, who wanted nothing more than sex from me that one and done kind of thing. I learned so much about learning to respect my body because I allowed it to be used by others too many times with nothing to show for my efforts but failed or no relationship. The root cause to my pain was me trying to be someone other than who I was trained and called to be in life.

To each person who purchased this book, I don't believe that you will be disappointed. If you are seeking direction, remember the word of God says we are overcomers through our testimonies. So, this is a testimony of all God has done in my life, choices I had to make and changes I applied to become the woman I am today.

I pray that the words on these pages will speak to you and your spirit, encourages you to move and take action in the areas that God is speaking to you for change in the same manner he called me to change. Remember we are 2 Peter 2:9 –"We are called out of Darkness into his marvelous light"…

This book is one that is real, transparent and possibly more direct than other books you will read and it an act of obedience to God on my part. It is not written with the intent of slandering, bashing, bragging, airing laundry or meeting others expectations. It is written for those that are seeking truth from a leader. Because of feeling a need for transitioning and transformation in your life but unsure of how to begin. Just make the choice to follow Christ Jesus, to trust him, and obey his word.

The beautiful thing about this book is I know I was called to write it, I am honored that God chose me to reveal, expose and share how He (God) removed me from all the things that was hindering me from becoming the woman He has called me to be in order for me to truly become the woman of God I am today. No one is too damaged emotionally, physically or spiritually, too broken, to be healed. No one is too sinful to be delivered. No one is too anything that God will not love them, heal them and deliver them through Christ Jesus. For you to know the love, experience the love, healing and deliverance I have grown to cherish, you must make a choice, you must make up in your mind – Enough is Enough of living outside the will of God. I want to live the life that God has designed for me, it is then in that moment my friend that the most amazing journey of your life will begin. Then you will know what it is to be the person God Intended You to Be!

Be blessed.
Dr. Tacoma R. Anderson

CHAPTER 1
Steps to Becoming

The first and greatest step to becoming the man or woman that God has called you to be is to first accept Christ into your life, as your Lord, Savior and King. That simple step will open the door to the greatest journey of your life on this side of heaven. You may wonder how can I make that step?

The first step to realize that you can't do this on your own, and you must be willing to repent of your sins according to Luke 13:5. Second, you must believe that Christ is the Son of God who died and was raised again for the remission of your sin found in John 3:16. 3. Accept Christ in as your Lord and savior according to Romans 10:13.

A simple prayer or faith confession : Lord, I am a sinner who needs your guidance and forgiveness. I believe that you are the Most high God, that your Son Jesus shed his blood for my sins on Calvary and arose again that I may have life everlasting with you, I desire that you live in me, please renew my spirit, mind and soul to be used for your purpose and glory. I believe you to be my Lord, my Savior and my deliver and I receive you in my life, so that I can be a son of God according to John 1:12, I know that through your spirit I am a new creation and the old things are passed away as stated in 2 Corinthians 5:17.

Dr. Tacoma R. Anderson

The Initial Steps

My process began at the age of 8 years old. I grew up in an Apostolic Pentecostal Holiness church, the old timers would call it the age of Fire and Brimstone because that is what was taught mostly was the need to get your house in order or you're going to die and go to hell.

I was in church one Sunday morning with my dad and the message was a little different from the other services, this one was talking about the love of God and how he desires to have a relationship with you as a person, how he loves you and wants you to have a life that is full of greatness, abundance of peace and joy. I don't know about you but I have always longed for joy and peace in my life. I felt the pull of the Holy Spirit and walked up to the front I think I was the first person on the alter and I don't remember if it was even alter call time or not, I do remember that I wanted to have God in me, living in me, teaching me and guiding me and I surely didn't want to live in hell for eternity.

That was one of the most important choices I made in my life, it is truly the greatest spiritual choice I made. I wanted the new life in Christ that the preacher had spoken about. That January 9th, 1979 was the first step to becoming the person I am today. That day because of my choice, my dad rededicated his life to Christ. Why? Because he wanted to be a true role model for his daughters and if his eight-year-old realized she needed Christ, then he needed to be able to guide her. Isn't God amazing, how a child can lead a parent to the glory of God because of the love in their heart to want the best for the child. I remember my Dad saying, that if I was going to live the life of a Christian, he must set the example. I really didn't understand the word of God that well, I read the word just to be reading pretty much. I always felt that my Grandmothers' prayed too long, but I did want to be like them in the fact they could quote scripture accurately from the word of God. I realized that they had the word of God hidden in their heart, as described in **1 Peter 3:4:**

But let it be the **hidden** man of the **heart**, in that which is not corruptible, even the ornament of a meek and <u>quiet</u> spirit, which is in the <u>sight</u> of God of great price.
1 Peter.

My grandmothers had been like : **John 5:39**

You diligently study the Scriptures because you think that by them you possess eternal life. These are the Scriptures that testify about me,

I also realized how my Dad begin to study his word even the more. When he began studied, he also began to turn away from the people who he would smoke and drink with, he followed the leading of God through his word in

Psalm 1:1 Blessed is the man that walketh not in the counsel of the **ungodly**, nor standish in the way of sinners, nor sitteth in the seat of the scornful.

My Dad actually had separated himself from those who were not following Christ, he taught my sister's and I about

1 Peter 4:18 And if the righteous scarcely be saved, where shall the **ungodly** and the sinner appear?

I remember getting baptized at Moring Star Church in Wytheville, VA, it was on a Saturday night in March 1979. After I went down in the water, I remember coming up and going back to the pews, and the jubilee service continued I was one of five that was baptized that night. As the song of praise went forth the Holy Spirit came into the mist of the Sanctuary. I remember it so well, I saw 3 angels in the room two to the front and one to my rear, it could have been more but I remember the room being illuminated. The word of God came forth through the Prophet that was present. There was a person speaking in tongues and another was interrupting the tongues as spoken of in

1 Corinthians 12:10: To another the working of miracles; to another prophecy; to another discerning of spirits; to another divers' kinds of **tongues**; to another the interpretation of **tongues**:

1 Corinthians 14:5
I would that ye all spake with **tongues** but rather that ye prophesied: for greater is he that prophesieth than he that speaketh with **tongues**, except he interpret, that the church may receive edifying.

During the next few months, I was in the mist of prophets, more than I can remember. I remember being back at Little Zion (Taylor's Chapel) and being called to the front by the Prophet of God, and the word came forth that I was Chosen to do the work of God, that I was gifted in many areas of my life and that I could play any instrument I touched because my love for music was that strong.

Deuteronomy 7:6
For thou art an holy people unto the LORD thy God: the LORD thy God hath **chosen** thee to be a special people unto himself, above all people that are upon the face of the earth.

Deuteronomy 14:2
For thou art an holy people unto the LORD thy God, and the LORD hath **chosen** thee to be a peculiar people unto himself, above all the nations that are upon the earth.

Matthew 22:14
For many are called, but **few** are **chosen**.

I didn't truly realize how special I was to God even then. See, I never fit in with the crowd, I was considered a friend to all, but I was always different from the rest. I was in a backslidden state of mind because I had given in to the peer pressures. Even then as I reflect on my writings, my relationship with God was evident. I referred to God in almost all my writings about how He brought me through. Funny, as a teen you don't often realize what you are experiencing is actually spiritual moments or revelation. My Dad knew God had his hands on me when I started sharing with him my dreams, and I was prophesying even as a child even though I didn't know it. All I knew was I had dreams, some good some bad that I shared with my dad and they were coming to pass just as I dreamed them.

Job 7:14
Then thou scarest me with dreams, and terrifiest me through **visions**:

Daniel 4:5
I saw a dream which made me afraid, and the thoughts upon my bed and the **visions** of my head troubled me.

Joel 2:28
And it shall come to pass afterward, that I will pour out my spirit upon all flesh; and your sons and your daughters shall prophesy, your old men shall dream dreams, your young men shall **see visions**:

Acts 2:17
And it shall come to pass in the last days, saith God, I will pour out of my Spirit upon all flesh: and your sons and your daughters shall prophesy, and your young men shall **see visions**, and your old men shall dream dreams:

The Lord was speaking to me through my dreams, I even remember being 14 and having a dream of casting out demons, walking with Christ and the message that was repeated was "it is time to fight the battle, you must put on the whole armor of God, it is time to fight the battle"

Ephesians 6:11
Put on the whole **armour** of **God**, that ye may be able to stand against the wiles of the devil.

Ephesians 6:13
Wherefore take unto you the whole **armour** of **God**, that ye may be able to withstand in the evil day, and having done all, to stand.

I remember my Dad laughing, that was his way of trying to remove the fear that I was experiencing from the dream. However, he began a deeper impartation of the word of God in me after that day. I was scared then but the dream and the words God spoke that night has never left me even to this day. I didn't realize just how closely I was walking with God at that time. I know this thing is so true, God said he will never leave you nor forsake you. I have been through somethings that will have people's mouth dropping in disbelief and I am sure some will feel I am lying just to sell a book that is not the case here. I pray that God will show you just how He will protect and keep his children even when they are trying to rebel in order not to be used because of allowing their emotions to control them.

As a young woman leaving home at the age of 17, I had so many dreams, my desire was to travel the world and experience all the cultures I read about in History or saw on National Geographic magazines and TV. So, for me to do that I decided to join the Army four days after high school graduation. I knew that the military was all over the world, because I heard my dad speak about his travels when he was on active duty and of course the commercials really enticed my desire "To Be All You Can Be".

Honestly, joining the military was one of the best decisions I could have made, it enhanced my character. My time in service molded me into a more rounded verses self- consumed person. I grew greatly during assignments stateside, overseas tours and my short deployment in Somalia. I quickly had to face spiritual, emotional and ethical conflicts within my career and relationships. There were a lot of dark periods in this journey, but in those periods of darkness, no matter how bad the depression or the situation got, my only one source of comfort was Christ Jesus. I didn't understand why I was going through the challenges that I was, nor did I enjoy them, but God used them to mold me into the woman I am today. Yes, that is something you will hear me repeat, over and over, my life as a woman of God has been a continual process of making and molding, reshaping my heart, realigning my emotional responses and my mind to not accept the things that our society says is or should be, but follow the moral compass inside of me. That compass is the Holy Spirit that draws me closer to the throne of God than away from it.

I have to say this, I PRAISE AND THANK GOD for loving me and keeping me even when I desired to die! My life wasn't what I felt like it should be I was battling a series of events that were like falling dominoes. I had lost my career for not meeting a standard of weight, my long-term relationship abruptly ended. I was overwhelmed with debt due to unemployment. I didn't make the type of money I once made. I was lonely. I allowed others to speak in my life and I believed lies that didn't align with my purpose or my call. I had felt betrayed by my employer, so called friends and even someone I trusted in ministry.

During this season of breaking and remolding into God's image is where God begin to restore in me the right mind and right spirit.

God humbled me and brought me to an understanding that the things of this world was not what I needed to live for at all. That the possessions of life should not possess me. I should not be obsessed with materialism the way I was in my late teens and early twenties. I will go more into detail about most of this later in this book, but just to let someone who is dealing with depression, suicidal ideations know you can overcome this situation. You have too much to live for than you do to die over.

Trust and believe there were so many things that were drawing me away from God, that was of my own lust and desires. Yes, Lust! I was full of it then, and I am not ashamed to tell it. I rejoice today because God not only has healed me - I am delivered from it too!

See, when God delivers you from something, it is such a wonderful thing that you are not ashamed to say where you been because you know you are not there anymore. Reflect on when you were so excited to go from elementary, to middle, to high school. Then for some of us it was the work force, others it was college but each was as stage you reflected and was grateful you had come through. When God delivers you from a sinful process and mindset you get the same excitement and you have the same mentality. I thank God I never have to go to High school again praise!

It was because of the call on my life that I had such a desire to go to the nations. The ministry God has established in me has always taken me to the nations. First in the early 90's when I got to go to Asian nations and middle eastern and European countries. In 2010, I had really decided to stop running from God, and run to him instead. I decided to finally do things His way because my way ended in failure every time. I was sick and tire of being sick and tired of how things were going my way. I desired a better life emotionally and spiritually for myself and those in my life.

Keep in mind that God had already begun this process of renewing my mind and vision in 2008. It all started Jan 26, 2008 at approximately 615 pm. I remember how it felt the day and moment I knew my daddy was no longer with me. We all know that day is destined to come when we will not see the ones, we love the most whether it be it we expire or they expire. My dad was the closest person to me, he was my best friend, my spiritual advisor, my confidant and my greatest source of encouragement and challenge. When it was confirmed that dad was no longer on this side of Glory, I began to notify my siblings, my mother and other family members. As the time passed everyone who knew me began to move in as a hedge of protection and comfort. God even sent an angel to minister to me in the form of a friend to help me to focus on the important things and not the responsibilities I knew my dad had bestowed on me. When I would receive calls people were expecting me to be in tears and all broken, when they asked how are you? My response was I am ok, I know that for God to take my dad, He (God) is taking me to a place where I must rely totally on him, a place my Dad could not lead me. I can't allow anyone else to have input in my choices, I must seek God for all things.

This was a profound moment for me and everyone that heard it. Why? because there were several people that were so focused on my sin life, and perceived relationships that they were to blind to see the transformation God was doing in me. I had to trust God regardless of what others thought was going on in my natural life, or relationships with friends and family. Yet, in the most difficult moment in my life to this point, God had truly become my focus. God was my strength and healing began immediately. I wish that more people can develop and nurture their relationship with their natural fathers and mothers while they have the time. It's time to put aside all things that is causing the family division. Even, as close as I was to my dad, God reminded me that He loved me even more than he ever could. I knew my dad would give his last everything for me. God gave His only son for me and you to be redeemed to His kingdom.

Life is truly about sacrifice, transformation and transitioning into a greater place of peace and understanding of who you are an what your purpose is in life.

All through life you learn to sacrifice your desires to either help or make other people's life a little easier. You may sacrifice time set aside for housework, gym or just a little me time to keep your sanity to help a neighbor, a friend or work in your community. Often time, we give so much of ourselves that we begin to neglect ourselves.

Sacrifice doesn't require you to ever neglect yourself! If you are in a position where you are feeling your time is being obligated without your consent speak up. If you don't you are condoning and eventually allowing your inability to speak up concerning your own need for time to eventually develop into resentment. We as people often get so caught up in over working ours. That is not what life is intended to be like at all. We are to enjoy our tender moments with God, people and ourselves. Time is our most precious commodity because it only spends once. If we are always over worked, overwhelmed then we become unloving, and unenjoyable beings. Take time to be the better you, soak in the tub, get the massage, pedicures, take the drive in the car to somewhere, and nowhere in particular. Do what makes you feel beautiful and at peace with the wonderful creation you are inside and out.

CHAPTER 2
Don't Count Me Out

It is amazing that I still remember the days when I was young and my dad was now a single father due to life choices. I remember hearing the grown people's conversations behind his back saying that he would never make it as a single dad. I remember hearing what I know now as "word curses" being spoken over him and his three girls.

People, to include family were saying that we would all be wild (loose women), that we would never have anything in life and that we would have a house full of babies and never graduate from high school. There were so many rumors and conversations on why my mom chose to leave. However, as I matured, I began to see it as a blessing and not a curse. It was because that decision was vital in the molding process of me becoming who I am today. That choice made me decide how I would be as a mother and what I would do if I was ever in her shoes. Sometimes when people exit our life it because of their love as well as our protection emotionally.

I thank God that my dad didn't feed into these demonic word curses that was spoken over him or my siblings and I, but he trusted God. There were so many times when my dad would be reading his bible and share the word of God with us. Times when things were hard financially and he would confess that this is not what God promised, and Lord I trust you to make a way, I going to this mailbox, and I expect to have money to feed my kids.

Guess what, there would be money. The beautiful thing about where I was raised as a child is that the community is family too. The other beautiful thing is that it was never about race and color where I was raised either. Even though our town also had its time of segregation. The little town of Fries, VA, is a place where my heart will always have love and cherished memories.

Why will I cherish a place that has little to offer? Because Fries, like many people in our life, has to so much offer and to give, but you must have eyes to see what they are able and willing to give. However, because it doesn't equate to the financial or physical things, we desire we frequently overlook it. I will always cherish my hometown and its people because they are my family too, and after the loss of my dad they reminded me I had other family besides my grandmother to come home too.

See, when my dad was raising the older three of the four of us, there were so many people who were there to help. Like our neighbors would plow the snow while my dad slept from his night shift, and my grandparents would watch us when we were too young to stay at home alone. Then there were my friend's moms who taught me about the facts of life as a maturing woman.

See my dad taught us important things that other places and people miss. Dad trusted in God to help get him through single parenting, and he taught us how to lean on God during all seasons and ask for help when we were in need.

Regardless of what challenges life was bringing our direction, dad reminded us that we were family, and mom will always be our mom, to love and respect her as such. Don't listen to what people say about you and dream, you can do anything you can think to do, as long as you trust God and not only in yourself.

So, now today as I am writing these words, dad has been gone for over ten years. However, before he passed, He saw two of his four children that he raised achieve both a master's & bachelor's degree from higher learning institutes. Since his passing, three of his daughters have Bachelors, two have master's degree, and those two started their

Doctorate degrees and one has completed. One has established their own business by faith in God. The oldest sister business that is still growing. We are all successful in our own ways, raising our own families and being a light to our communities just as our dad was to his co-workers and friends. I celebrate my sister's achievements.

The beautiful thing about this is that we are not the product of the poor choices of our parents. We are not the product of our errors, we are instead the product of each choice we made good, bad and indifferent. We all ensured that we didn't become the people that didn't see our worth or value. We trusted God to validate who we are now and still maturing into as women. We all chose to be the best moms that we could because that is the person we needed. Due to our mom's choice at that stage in life she was not assessible to us the way we desired.

I love my hometown and all the people there because they truly believe in the concept it takes a village to raise a child. Even though racism is alive now as it was then in that area of Virginia. It didn't stop us from being considered family to so many people in the town. I can tell you from experience of having friends who have just as many photos of me growing up with their children as my own family has of us. Family is more than those you are born too! Family is also those you grow to love and endure the hardships as well as the joyful moments in life. My friends in Fries, VA and some of their parents reminded me not to long ago, my family is more than my grandmother and my dad. They are my family as well which means I should come home more often to spend time with them too.

This is a blessing that most people never truly encounter. Some people never experiences being truly loved for being themselves and would be blessed to experience the love of family and the love of community.

CHAPTER 3
Lost Hope -I can't go on

It is just a couple of weeks after me hitting my mid-twenties. People around me think my life is all together and I am slowly dying inside my heart, my spirit, and it is trying to creep into my soul. Why, is my life in shambles, why did I have to lose my career, why am I being told I am overweight because I am one hundred and forty pounds. Why is he still cheating on me, Why! Why! Why! Why God!!! Why am I such a failure!

This was my head talking to me, I was in one of the most depressing seasons of my life and this was only the beginning as I look back on my journey. I had done everything I knew to do as being right. I was in the church, active in ministry as a missionary(traditional church) and amour bearer to my pastor, and yes, I was working a fulltime low paying job.

My life had drastically changed in the last two years, I went from being successful in my military career, honorable soldier, highly motivated to being discharged honorable over three pounds. I was so frustrated, I am waking in the night in cold sweats, heart pounding, reliving things that happen during my deployment, noises make me think someone is trying to break in and this sexual relationship is plagued by cheating and it was time to relocate to another state with the military, I have to sale this house.

I am so overwhelmed with my life, that I felt the only person who truly loved me was my Dad, and I was making our phone calls shorter and shorter as I tried to stay upbeat. See if anyone could see through me it was Dad, he knew when I was in pain, trouble and really going through because of our spiritual connection since my birth. My dad was my world and a meaningful loving relationship was all I wanted, hoping to be a mother one day. I had once again made my relationship with a man, the god in my life. How did I do that, I focused more on trying to save my unhealthy relationship with someone who was not ready to totally commit to me, or at least in the same manner I was committed. Not to say that he was totally wrong he was following the footprint laid before him in life following his desires. I was at a place where I was trying to make someone love, respect and desire to be with me that didn't. I had invested my whole self once again into a sexual encounter that never evolved into a real meaningful relationship.

I knew that his desire to be involved with me had ended shortly after I returned from overseas. In all honesty we should have ended our sexual encounter and not try to pursue anything before I deployed. I was home after my redeployment and I had a nightmare of the things that happen while I was gone, and when I awoke, I looked to find an empty space next to me, he wasn't there, which sent me into a panic, because now both places are running in my head and I am not sure if I am in Africa or the states, I walk around the house and he is nowhere to be found. A few hours later he walks in the door and says, some crazy lie that yes, I believed. Then a few days later, I am out with one of my two battle buddies, and we are at the gas station getting gas, and my lover at the time pulls up and is pumping gas for this pregnant woman. He is talking to my friend, I hadn't noticed him, (I was so green=naive) when he spoke, he said he was helping his friend's wife while he was on duty. I am from the country in Virginia, that is what neighbors do, so I thought nothing of the situation. Then my battle, ripped into me as we were pulling off, and told me I need to be more aware of what was going on, that woman looked like she was with him and not someone else, open your eyes little girl, and you will know the truth.

That comment was so on point, on my birthday that year, my perfect world in my eyes took the hit that would last the duration of our time as together. That same woman came to my house and demanded to see my lover, this is his baby, and if you don't let me see him or I will go to the base commander and tell the whole story and he will be kicked out the service. I immediately went to start fighting her, because all the hurt, betrayal, disbelieve, disrespect really angered me so much. Then without warning BAM! I was hit straight in my face right in front of this woman. How could he do such a thing and how could he treat her like they were together and I was the side chick? I felt like Sarah in that moment, I was told I couldn't have children when I was eighteen, and here this woman is carrying my then lover's baby and it was conceived during the while I was deployed. I tried to rationalize the situation and keep him from losing his job and a trying to understand why this is happening? How could God allow this to happen to me! All of us at some time or another has asked these types of questions to God.

Well, If I was discerning and not just flowing in my emotions at the time after I prayed that God show me if this is the man, I should be with I would not have gotten involved with him. God always answers prayer of the righteous. We must be in the place where we accept the answer when it comes. When my answer came three times, I didn't receive it because of how it was packaged. The first response came from two of my military brothers, I knew their lifestyle and didn't take heed. The second time, came from a female servicemember I was supposed to share a room within the barracks, but I resided off base. This young lady came to me and I was receptive until she stated, "he is not the one for you, He can never love you like I do or will." I went from zero – one twenty with my temper. I told that young lady if she ever propositions me, I would beat the life out of her. I have a Peter spirit – I will fight at the drop of the dime.

The third was a subtle comment that I didn't really look deeper into but should have because it was a seed of betrayal before I ever got deeply involved with him. The young lady who was my close friend, told me that she once lost a close friend because she had an intimate relationship with her friends' husband. I grew up with the understanding that people can repent and be forgiven, like the woman at the well and not sin that way again. I overlooked that she was trying to tell me she had sex with the man I was involved with and had once thought I would marry.

The crazy thing is that this is not the first time I was involved in a relationship that had the potential for abuse. I was at one of my stateside locations for training before going overseas and I was in another long-term military relationship. We were into the party scene, and this one particular night we were both in the club but not together hanging with the people we were close too. He got upset, because I was not patient for him to tell me what was on his mind as he played a video game. We agreed to chill with our crews and meet up later that night to enjoy time together. We are both on the dance floor dancing with other people fast songs, when a slow song comes on and this girl is a little to close for my liking. I asked to cut in, and he was being spiteful to make me jealous and said no, when she asked if I was his girlfriend, he said no. I cut in between them and asked him if I am not your girlfriend then who am I? Then, the unthinkable, in my anger, I ripped his shirt and demanded that we talk about what was going on. I learned that my temperament would be a downfall to me having a healthy meaningful relationship in my future. After all, we were together so much that everyone around us just knew that we were destined for marriage to each other before we went overseas.

Because of my lack of discernment, I experienced a lot of emotional and physical duress because I didn't recognize the word of God because of who was sent to deliver the message. I had put all my faith in a men and not in the creator who was sending me warning. Even my dad said, Tacoma, he has wondering eyes- country slang for he is one that will cheat.

God is amazing because during this process of being unequally yoked with my former lover on what is expected in a monogamous relationship, faith, spending /saving money. God used it to show me who I was in him. I had believed so many lies that others had spoken about me; some conversations people don't even know I heard that made me doubt my natural and spiritual identity.

After that and other failed short and long-term encounters over the next decade, I went the emotional bungy jumps of the joys of being in love, to extreme depression with melancholy, suicidal ideations and even planning my own death because I had put my hope and trust in the wrong place. I put unrealistic expectations on men to love me the way that only God could. The only way a person can love you as God is that have to have an intimate relationship with God to share the love, he has placed in them for you. I had to realize that everyone is not a true neighbor like those I grew up with who had integrity and respect for couples regardless of their marital status or friendships in general.

I was so disappointed with myself for allowing myself to be made a fool of, I was vexed with shame about how often I had stayed in a dead-end sexual relationship with and what was going on in my life. I beat myself up for years feeling that there was something wrong with me that I was not enough, I had some defect that caused the men I was with to cheat on me. I did everything in my earthly power to try and save my relationships in the past – the thing I had made my god.

Just like so many times before the end came, it was inevitable, this person stood in my face and told me he never loved me, I was a challenge, I was nothing more than a trophy to him. He didn't care who made passes at me, I was like dog poop on his shoe by the end of our involvement. The women were so many I stopped counting. I realized the hard way, you can't make a man love you, respect you or stay with you if he desires to be somewhere else and children surely don't change that equation either. Because of insecurities and issues of abandonment, I found myself trying to force sexual encounters with the men I would be involved with into a wholesome relationship.

By the final days of one particular relationship the frustration and resentment grew in a bad way, so much so that abuse verbal and physical occurred that we fought with a loaded weapon, by the grace of God, I was able to get out of the place we were at and neither one of us was hurt. He was removed from the building at gun point and I was blessed that our lives were spared Praise God. The blessing is we all made it out alive. There are so many relationships between men and women who have been involved for months and sometimes years where the emotions get so high, the bitterness and resentment that it leads to the same violence with a different ending.

One of the most powerful things God every said to me that impacted and changed me was.... Your wrath is nothing compared to mine.

Then he brought to my remembrance the scripture Galatians 5:7-10 but we will focus on Verse 7 "be not deceived; God is not mocked: for whatsoever a man sowthe, that shall he also reap"

In my youth and early 20's I was all about getting revenge. However, at this particular point in my life, God began to show me that everything I was doing to show others my strength was only bringing destruction into my own life.

At this moment in time, I was really hurting, feeling betrayed and stupid for believing in a lie that was longer than some peoples lifetime. However, I cried out to Christ Jesus like Jeremiah 33:3 was saying and here God began to give me knowledge and understanding of what it really means the battle is not mine but the Lords.

For this instance, there is no need to go into the mess of what transpired but a need to focus on the growth that took place in my personal walk. God showed me that Love truly does cover a multitude of sin. It also covers and destroys pain and suffering when you surrender it to God for healing.

I was not only ridiculed, talked about behind my back and even some boldly to my face, stating that I wasn't a true woman because of how I chose to handle the situation. Instead of seeking counsel from those who appeared to have it all together, or my girl if I were you corner, I turned to the only person I knew I could always trust with my deepest thoughts and pain. I turned to God in prayer, and reading the bible, the words began to come to life for me as I read scriptures in Psalms and in Jeremiah.

I chose to walk away from the temptation of causing destruction into someone's life, even though I had all kinds of evidence to really wreak this person's career and personal life for years. God showed me where I would be in life, if he chose not to forgive me of all I did wrong against him. He reminded me that He was my first true love, and He will always love me regardless of who doesn't love me.

One again, I shared this to encourage you, God will make a way of escape, he didn't call you to be anyone's punching bag and the man /

woman He has for you will always desire the best for you, and there is no sorrow attached to the blessing of God.

By the time we acknowledged the path of unnecessary destruction we were one, we amicable ended our encounter with a few laughs of our good moments shared with friends and a kiss goodbye, wishing each other the best. We both realized we could be friends and nothing more. We have asked and given forgiveness to our individual parts of this painful process. However, look at what God has done, that we can forgive, forget and move forward with mutual respect and our relationships. We are all better people because we chose to let God heal us of our past, we all chose to let go of the hurt, the anger, bitterness and the pain, we chose to live our lives in peace. Nothing and No one But GOD made that possible!

CHAPTER 4
Hope Defeats Suicide

The time was late October 1997, I was out of the military now about fifteen months or so and life was a lot of a challenge. God had blessed me with a job that paid more than minimum wage, but the people failed to give me all the things promised in the interview and since It was not a written contract it was as if the things promised didn't exist.

I worked over forty miles from my home and the hours away at times could be twelve or more hours at a time. I was living a life full of broken dreams and I was so alone. To me the worst place to be in a relationship is to feel like you are alone while being involved with someone. I was at a point where depression from all the things that I had allowed to pile up over the years begin to weigh heavily in my thoughts.

There were so many struggles in my mind. I blamed myself for losing my career in the Army for failing to meet weight control standards, even though I was experiencing medical issues that were not considered serious enough to cause the inability to lose weight. I was under a lot of stress at work and home. The only peace I had was when I was with my son reading his books or in a church service and the presence of God was there to wrap me in his arms like described in Psalms 91.

Our home had experienced severe damage from a hurricane two days after our one year of living in it, so I was stuck with trying to sale a home, relocate to another state, and me finding a job that will help with the bills.

My pay was cut in half from my time in the military and the drive was brutal but it covered my son's childcare and gas back and forth to work. Our house was going into foreclosure, and I could not afford to do it all alone with my income.

I was having severe anxiety attacks pertaining to my safety, it was just a seriously rough time in life. I decided that the best thing for me to do was to take my life, at least it would be enough to get my family out of debt. I knew my son would not have to suffer in poverty. I was in a place where I was tired of trying to make it work, trying to get promotions where the deck was stacked against me because of favoritism and racism. I was tired of being alone, I was tired of hurting and tired of feeling like life was being sucked out of me. The crazy thing is I was functioning as if there were no issues in my life. There was only one person who picked up spiritually that something wasn't right and that was my dad. I knew how close we were so I keep those conversations really short and sweet and they became less than every day too. I told Dad, I had extra things going on with the church.

Yes, you can be in the church, servicing in ministry and not surrendered all your cares to the Lord and be vexed with the spirit of depression, isolations, which are open doors for suicidal idealizations. Which is where I was in life. I had held so much in that I was at the point it was time to end it all. That was the only way that I could perceive being free from the downward spiral of hell that my life had become. It seems like everything I cared about was gone, so why live? I was in a state of desperation.

My dad had earlier in the year prior had recommend that I seek mental health assistance from the VA because he could see the impact that all these major life changes were having on my life. I remember telling the counselor how I was feeling and as I was talking getting the impression they really weren't listening. I felt as if it was wasting my time. I shared with them the year before I got out of service about how I was having dreams of causing harm to other people who had been harassing me. I had this overwhelming pressure, that I needed to relief from, and yet I felt as if no one heard me or was listening. The guy told me I was suicidal, I stated to him I am not trying to cause harm to myself! If anything, I was homicidal because I wanted the people to leave me alone at any cost and I am dreaming of causing them harm. I was able to walk out of that VA office with nothing said to me, and the crazy thing, there is no record of that happening on the VA's account. I wonder how many other veterans have encountered those type of people in their treatment.

None the less, as time passed, I didn't see how it would benefit me to go where I am not heard, I hate to waste my time and breathe. So, without even really realizing I began to become fixated on dying. To the point that I developed a plan that I was soon to execute. I just wanted it to be a beautiful day. I wanted the day to reflect the peace I had in my decision to kill myself. I just didn't want my son to be in the house when it happened.

By this time, It was about my birthday, and a close friend from Korea that I had served with gave me a call. He said God had put me on his heart and he was praying for me, and he asked if everything was okay. I told him I was placing the home for sale and relocating shortly after to a new life. He knew how I felt about being near my family in Virginia and keeping together because he was around me when I was overseas.

My friend told me T, If you don't sale your house by this date...I will buy it. He had never been to my house but he knew my taste so he was okay with it. That moment gave me a little hope to continue pressing through for a while. Then things got so tight I went on a continual fast because I could not afford to pay the utilities, childcare, and gas back and forth to work. The harder it got the more I determined my best course of action was to commit suicide.

It was late October early November time frame and it was unseasonably warm out. I decided this is it, it was the most beautiful sunrise I had seen in a long time, the air was fresh and everything around me was at peace. I said today is the best day to die. So, I began to implement my suicide plan. I called the other babysitter, a lady from church and told her I was preparing the house for sale, I needed to shampoo the floors and I didn't want the baby to catch cold and asked her to watch him for me. She agreed to watch him, all I had to do was get him there. I had already shampooed the floors; the house was spotless. I just needed to get my son to a safe place, so he would not be scared by the impact of my decision.

I decided it was no need for any explanation of my actions, those who I loved knew I loved them and those who had rejected me knew where we stood as well. I was at peace with the decision. I had just got the baby strapped into the car seat and was about to pull off when my friend was standing next to my window. I promise it was an angel in the form of my friend, as he said he could not account for how he even got there. He asked me to go to church revival that night. Knowing my plan, I said, we will see what the Lord allows for the day, no promises. I said anything to get him to leave so I could return and kill myself. Anyway, my friend talked to me so long that the babysitter was not home. I had no choice but to wait another time. I did go to church that night and when praying I felt a little release from the pressure of the weight I was trying to carry on my own.

Then the minister began to speak, he had my address in the spirit, he spoke about everything I was going through that day and told me God keep me for his purpose. I cried out like never before to the lord that night and let it all go.

My friend did buy my home and we were closer to family. I held on so hard trying to give my son what I didn't have and it was killing me not only emotionally but spiritually as well.

I realized that God had a purpose for me and he reminded me that my life is not my own to take. I thank God for deliverance from suicidal ideations. I have battled with the thoughts for years, until one day I decided to take God at his word. I will not walk in fear, I will live and not die to proclaim the works of the Lord according to Psalms 118:17.

I had to learn to make this a part of my faith confession. I remember telling one of the psychologists that I didn't have a mental health disorder. I was one of the few people who seen the reality of life and not living through rose colored glasses and the state of the world caused me to be sad, there was so much unnecessary evil done to others. There is no longer a regard for life and it's so much hate that it is heavy to watch and be a part of it.

I now realize that because of my call on my life, that I have compassion for the people of God. I hurt when I see the state of the world. I began to live a life of intercessory prayer crying out on behalf of Gods people to not die early, to be strengthen, to not be murdered, to come out of adultery, to come out of darkness into the marvelous light like he had delivered me.

I thank God for not giving up on me when I felt there was no good in my life to live for other than my son. I was so full of pain, that at times I felt he would be better without me. That was a lie straight from the pits of hell. I had to stop entertaining the vain imaginations and the satanic whispers of inadequacies in my life. I had to take God at his word and speak about who his word says I am! I had to walk in the divine appointed and anointed call on my life.

I never thought that running from my destiny would cause me to try to run to a natural death. Anytime you are not moving in the will of God you are operation in spiritual death that will try to take you into a natural death like the one I had purposely planned by suicide.

Even years after I had become by societies terms successful with a high salary career, a good child who was honor student. I still failed at having a healthy God ordained relationship that I so strongly desired. I was back in that depression / suicidal place again. The stress from bills, demands and expectations of others, and it seemed like no one was concerned about me or my happiness. It just seemed like everyone was treating me like an atm machine, making withdrawals and not making any deposits in my life to encourage or strengthen me. That Christmas my son's girl friend had noticed all the small rocks in the house that had words of affirmation on them and she gave me a small box with a rock "Hope". That little rock was like a love letter from God to me, because I felt like he was trying to get me to not lose hope. In addition to the rock, I was studying my word and I ran across this scripture: Proverbs 13: 13 Hope deferred makes the heart sick, but a longing fulfilled is a tree of life.

I decided that day to live on purpose. I refuse to die without fulfilling the dreams and visions God had placed in my spirit as a child. I choose to live on purpose now, and when things get hard, I remind myself of these words and Jeremiah 29:11. I know that God has made me to be a Victor and not a victim. I choose to live a victorious life for the rest of my life in Jesus name! The hardest part about dealing with someone who has what society classifies as a mental health issue is trying to get them to realize that they are being heard. That they are being taken seriously and bring some type of relief to their mental anguish by some means other than drugs that intensify the suicidal thoughts. We don't need to lose another person to suicide because they feel there is no way out.

I thank God for his healing and deliverance from suicide, I bind up all suicidal thought and ideas that is trying to vex your spirit. I command every voice of the enemy to be silenced and the only voice you will hear is the voice of the Holy Spirit that has come to comfort you and bring peace to every area in your life. I pray that you will submit your spirit to the guidance of the Holy Spirit that you can be led by him during this season of darkness in to the light of God's glory and I declare Psalms 118: 17 over your life that you shall live and not die and you shall proclaim the work that the Lord has purposed for your life in Jesus name. amen.

CHAPTER 5
My life is in A Holding Pattern

So, what do you do when you feel like your life is in a holding pattern? What do I mean by that statement? Airplanes will hold their flight pattern when there is a delay in their ability to land because they have not obtained permission from the Air Traffic Controller. They are in a state or period of no progress and may at times have to circle around the landing stripe area until they get permission to land.

So, what do you do when you feel like regardless of what you are doing your life still seems to be either in continual chaos or no movement? I know what that is like oh to well. I felt that way in different seasons in my life seeking a better job, wanting a real relationship and trying to be where God has called me verses living a life of promiscuity.

Even though I didn't see it then, when I was crying out in prayer. God had given me a special grace to endure and preserve through the toughest times of my life. Perseverance to endure things that would cause other people to commit suicide or homicide because of built up and unaddressed anger and resentment.

So, why was I in that place where I could not move forward? I was there to resolve the issues that were stumbling blocks in my way. I had to let go of the old things, the hurt, the unforgiveness, the resentment, and I needed to be humbled to tell the truth.

I found that after I identified with my role in the hardships, I was experiencing that I was angrier at myself for being there in the first place. I found it hard to forgive myself for not moving sooner, and not using my common sense God had given me. I should not ever had gotten myself or stayed in a place of physical, emotional, mental abuse, neglect, low pay and dead churches.

I remember what it was like going through the verbal, emotional, mental and physical abuse in between the good times. I tried so hard to be everything to everyone that I was around trying to ensure they would love me because of what I did. Hoping that they would see who I was to them. So much that I almost lost the essence of who I am. I was doing so much in the church and work to compensate for what I didn't have at home waiting for me. Even with that I was in that holding pattern where I wasn't moving in ministry, I wasn't moving on the dead-end job and regardless of how much I spoke to the dryness of sexual encounter it was already dead or dying. I found myself dying inside too, however there was a part of me that refused to die in the Midwest. I refused to let go of the promises that I had read in God's word.

I was in the Carolinas, attending a church their prior to my relocating to the Midwest. There was a guess minister there, and I was singing an old song "I feel no ways tired", She asked, why are you so young and singing a song like that? I looked at my relationship that died in the first few months. I looked at the job that I was working that deceived me. I looked at the church that seemed to focus on other things more than they focused on the souls. I just knew that if could I reminded myself that as I am climbing up on the rough side of the mountain; I should not feel tired. I had to Press my way through. I had to persevere for my change to come, just like the woman with the issue of blood in Matthew 9:20-22, I had to get to the presence of the one who had the ability to change my circumstances.

So, I am praying and I am fasting, trusting and believing yet it still seems like nothing is happening. What is really going on Lord? God was doing his perfect work in me. That is what is going on, and that is what is going on with you, if you are in that place. God wants to heal us before He allows us to go into places that will agitate the woundedness in our hearts. Once we have overcome then that thing that use to bother us will not affect us in the same manner. However, if we don't heal from the rejection of our path, we will see everything through the eyes of rejection even when it is a true redirection of our path by the grace of God.

I had to continually speak those things I desired, I spoke to the fact of my strength by not accepting becoming tired and weary. I had to know God for myself, not rely on what grandma' and "them" told me growing up. I had to get to know the God of the children of Israel. I needed a deliverance from the place of being stuck, oppressed, frustrated and loneliness. I knew that God would not allow me to stay in that place. I know that my life had greater in stored. I wanted to get moving toward it. So, one day, I just started crying out, Lord, I don't understand what is causing me to be here. I need to move forward. I need a change in the direction, something must give! Please help me! Lord, show me what I must do and I will do it!

Sometimes, we must get to the place in life where we realize that we can't do it all on our own. We don't always have the answers and understand that it is okay not having them. What we can't do in this season of being in a holding pattern is run out fuel. It is imperative to continue the course by not exhausting ourselves with trying to fix or control things that are not within our ability. This is the season where we must walk by faith and not by sight, regardless of what the things look like around you, speak the things you know God has in stored for your life!

During the season when my life was in a perpetual holding pattern, I had to declare I was not tired yet! I declared I will not get tired in my spirit. I will not let go of my faith in Christ Jesus. I will not accept less than what God has for me ever again!!!!!

My natural state of being was on a breaking point, I fought many days with thoughts of contemplating suicide. I had to choose to live each day and not die. I felt like I was on the end of a dangling frayed rope over a pit of scorpions and vipers ready to poison me to death. I was in a place where it seemed to be no end to the darkness in my life.

My life was that rope. I had to curtail my career aspirations, because the one I desired had diminished and ended abruptly. My relationship at that time was words only, no action. I was in the depths of a deep depression. At that point suicide seemed to be the way to bring peace and light to my darkness. That was a lie too. I had allowed my circumstance to control my outlook on life. I had begun to lose hope because I had become depending on my own abilities to make things work in life. When I finally hit a wall of my limitedness to control everything around me, I wanted to terminate the only thing real - my life.

I had to learn that God's will for my life was never to be in a place of oppression by my job, people or my faith. I learned to surrender all my desires to the desires that God had for me. I asked God if He would align not only my will but also my desires to His will and desires so I would not be out of his will at any time or pursue things that was not his will for my life.

That decision to pray that simple prayer, was a transitional point in my life. I began to see progress in the choices I made in my life. I got the promotion then relocated to be closer to family who could be used to strengthen my faith by the word continually and spending time together. I truly learned what it is to live the scripture Proverbs 10:22 KJV "The blessing of the Lord, it maketh rich, and he addeth no sorrow with it".

When I cried out to the lord and cast my cares to him according to Psalms 55:22 it began with humbling myself to allow God to have reign in my life. I had to trust in his ability to meet all my need according to Philippines 4:19 through Christ Jesus. I learned to guard my thoughts and my conversation. I learned to keep focused on the promises of God verses how I was feeling in my emotions or what I was seeing with my natural eyes. Each day I made the choice to live for Christ, to trust the process and to believe what I had prayed for was being released in my life.

Lord today for those who are feeling like their life is in a holding pattern, so much as that regardless of where they turn, it seems to be no way out of their situation. I am asking Lord that you will give them a peace of mind, send the Holy Spirit to comfort them in their distress. Lord, I am asking you to send your ministering angels out on their behalf, I dispatch them right now to go open the doors you have for them to walk through. To bring in the finances that are needed to sustain them. Lord, I thank you for pouring your spirit and your favor over and in their life that they will not have any dry places. That they have the favor of God in their life where people are concerned. Lord, I thank you for turning every tear sown in their distress into a bountiful harvest of joy, peace, love and the steadfast faith in you to do all that your word says. I thank you for teaching this reader today how to walk by faith, to trust your process, and to understand your will, your purpose and way for their life. In Jesus name.

CHAPTER 6
Still Not The One

Often, we meet someone and immediately jump into a sexual intimate relationship. Where the only thing you have is Sex! Yes, I have been there, that place where you are involved with a person and when things begin to happen that should cause the relationship to grow stronger, they disengage. The realization of not being intimate enough to grow through or work through the rough times is hard. Especially when you are emotionally vested in a person. Then without a real conversation or warning they drop the "it's time for me to move on, I just don't want nothing serious right now line. This usually happens when you desire more than the other person is willing to give or even capable of giving. Instead of taking the time to allow God to heal us from the last sexual encounter we seek comfort in someone else's bed. Yes, this is as real as real talk can get.

In the meantime, God is calling you to be holy and set yourself apart. You are running like water in the drain, going further away because you are not able to control your fleshly lust and emotional desire to be loved. I spent so many years, seeking in men what only God can give me. I spent too much time seeking validation from my lovers, be it prior to marriage, during marriage and after divorce. It wasn't until I realized by the other person moving forward with out me, I was given time to allow myself to get healing. I was able to become and stay focused on the person God was calling me to be verses the person who would cry for hours, days and months replaying all the what did I do wrong thoughts through my mind.

During this season of my life, I was so distracted by my own lust, just like James 1:14 states, that I could not see the hand of God moving in my life. I was in a place where I didn't value myself and allowed myself to be disrespected by the men, I chose to be intimate with continually. In fact, I allowed them to have just sex with me, no commitment, no accountability for their actions. Even when I forgave them for cheating or verbal comments that were disrespectful. My actions were more of desperation to have someone than actually having the experience of being loved by one. God was trying to show me the man He has for me would be in accordance with Proverbs 6:25, not lusting after my beauty in his heart. He would not be enticed by what I was wearing but how I was spiritually, emotionally.

So much of my time was spent trying to be a good woman, giving sex partners husband privileges. I spent a lot of time being depressed and oppressed with my feelings of inadequacy. It all stemmed from me investing my emotions into someone who was not investing in me.

I had so many mental conversations trying to heal from the breakup and seeing the other person moving on like I never existed. I was so distracted with these thoughts that I was not permitting myself to being healed from these disappointing moments. I second guessed who I was, my beauty, my value, my own self-worth because someone chose to walk away from me. I found myself constantly battling the spirit of rejection. The act of rejection. I was constantly traveling down the "WHY" road of destruction, emotional destruction. Asking myself questions like: Why didn't he see this as a good relationship? Why is it not working...? Why does he not want to be with me? What did I do wrong? Why is this happening to me? Why did he not see me as his future wife?

Instead of trusting that God had allowed this relationship to end because it is not aligned to my purpose. The purpose of being who He is calling me to be as a woman of faith, a woman of virtue and honor a proverbs 31 woman. As time went on, God began to open my understanding of who I am as a woman. He showed me my inner beauty, because I had invited Him in to dwell in my heart in my lowest moments. I began to praise Him at my highest, and even when things seemed to be dying especially my desire to love and be loved.

God began to do a new thing in my life. He revealed to me that my happiness is in Him, no one else's love could compare to His for me, not my dad, my son, my family, my lovers or my former or future husband. He showed me that true love and happiness is not dependent on another person it is within me! That others only can enhance or distract from who He created me to be in Him.

My prayer for you today is that you will surrender your brokenness to God. I pray that you will allow Him to heal the broken heart, the rejection, the unforgiveness inside you. I pray that God will release you for low self -esteem, feelings of inadequacy and bring you to a place of understanding that you are fearfully and wonderfully made in Him according to Psalms 139:14. I pray that the peace of God resonates in your life as you enter a season of restoration of your esteem in God, your identity in God and your relationship with God. That you will have the courage and the strength to wait on God to bring your healed mate to you in the appointed time that you will enjoy the best relationship known to you for a lifetime, this lifetime. In Jesus name.

CHAPTER 7
So, You Want a Bad Boy!

I remember the day I was at home cleaning the house and listening to music. I was thinking about the men that I had dated, before marriage and after my divorce some of whom people would characterize as Bad boys. I remember, hearing clearly this comment "So you want a bad boy! Well Get a bad boy in Christ!"

I began to laugh and smile. Then it hit me, we as woman (or men seeking woman) are constantly seeking after the person who will seem to bring us excitement. A person who will help us to feel like we are truly living life by living on the edge. We like having the unpredictable in our life because our life has become so ridge and schedule. We often feel like our lives is mundane to say the least.

God began to bring to my remembrance about the days I spent trying to have some thug passion in my life, that guy who was always on the edge of life. That guy that would not be tamed but was always moving fast. That person who would give me an emotional rush in the beginning but leave me emotionally depleted in the end. In my quest for having love, I was always willing to take that risk with the expectation that something was going to change.

The bad boys in my life also included that well-groomed brother, with the smooth conversation, the nice car who didn't mind wining and dining with you. I later learned that to him I was only a trophy on the arm for public display and a notch on his belt of all the women he conquered.

The consistent thing about these relationships was each one started fast and ended just as fast. These men in this type of relationship were never interested in anything about me the person, my mind, dreams or ideas. They weren't even concerned about wearing protection – it was only a sex thing. We were quick to move into becoming physically intimate with each other before even knowing the others last name.

This is no way to start any relationship. We moved so fast that we never discussed the sexual history or asked questions about any sexually transmitted disease history. In moments of lust we made irrational decisions that could have affected our life for the rest of our life. We could have impacted our lives through either transmitting of STDs or unplanned pregnancy. Walking in our flesh will keep us in a place where we are continually trying to please it.

It was during this season of life that I found myself trying to be everything other than what I was raised to be as a woman. I was trying my best to get away from everyone telling me I am acting like their wife. I found myself, seeking the worst bad boys I could find. I found myself being like a drug addict, except my addiction was for sex. I had one-night stands with strangers frequently. I was searching and finding men online that just wanted sex. I was constantly in sexually charged chat rooms. I found myself getting addicted to pornography and sex toys because of my involvement with some of the people. I was nothing to these men! My life felt empty and sex wasn't cutting it anymore either.

What I found happening was that I was seeking out new ways to feel pleasure. In doing so one day, I was going to have sex with a stranger. This guy, he was a true bad boy. This man was into some deep kinky sex, to include bondage. He had plans for me that I was unaware. God had something else planned for him. I had driven to his place and when he saw me, he had conviction in his heart. God will speak to you even in the middle of your sinful thought and acts. He spoke to me through this man who said, "What are you doing here? You know you could be killed by men out here, look at you, you are a church girl. I can tell, this is way out of your league, you are not ready for anything that I am into, you need to leave."Here, God had provided a way of escape for me, and I was so focused on sex that convinced the man to have sex. After all, I was going to walk the talk I had talked. We were going to meet my sexual craving before I left, besides the roads were in no condition for me to travel back home that night so I stayed. God protected me, there is no other way to say it than He protected his foolish child that He had given warning too. The man didn't do the things he planned because he became extremely sleepy. Looking back, I can praise God for His protection. I know my dad and other family members was praying for me during this season of rebellion, running from my call and looking for love in all the wrong men and places.

So, I responded back to God with "Okay, God, my way didn't work tell me what a bad boy in Christ is? Can you explain that one to me please?" Then God began to break it down to me what a bad boy in Christ is, he is a man that loves God with his whole heart and seeks his face like David. He is a man that has the discipline of Christ to pray and fast when others don't want to pray and fast. His priorities are to God, his family and then others. He is a man that is willing to go where God sends him. Because he is one that seeks his wisdom, instruction and direction from God. He is a man that can love his wife, because he sought her in the presence of God instead of for her physical attributes.

This is a man that is willing to pray for and with you. A man that can and will cover you in prayer. A man that will put fear into the kingdom of darkness because his love for God and his faith is deeply rooted in the word of God and God alone. His eyes are for the woman that has his heart and no other woman can tempt him and sway him away because he asked God for eyes only for his wife.

This is a man who when he accepts the total call on his life, can see the path God has designed for him. He is one who help others to see and join the vision. He is a pioneer, a pillar in his community and church. He is truly a man that is easy to submit to, for his love is in the heart of God. He is one who will build you up with his words, and not strike you with his hands.

He is a man who is not scared to follow his vision, to provide for his family and sees you as you were created as bone of his bone flesh of his flesh, for you are his rib. You are his helpmate.

So, I said, Lord, I would love to have someone like this in my life. So, where is he? Why has he not found me? What is taking him so long?

I had to realize that my timing was not God's timing. I had to realize that I was still full of baggage from my last relationship even though it never sailed. I had to be healed and delivered from all the soul ties I had created through sexual and emotional actions not just from my marriage but every relationship before and after that marriage. God had to do a deep cleaning and a deep healing in me to help me be in position for my Bad Boy in Christ to find me.

I had to get deliverance from the pornography movies, the sexual immorality, abandonment issues, being rejected and being in the shadow of past lovers' relationships. I had to be healed in my emotions, healed in my spirit and healed in my mind, and soul. I was on a very destructive path of moving too fast and not allowing myself to heal from past relationships.

When I think back on this promiscuous life that I was living before that transitional point in my life of choosing to serve God with all of myself. I am reminded of the book of Hosea; I was treating God the same way Gomer was treating Hosea. I was seeking after lovers everywhere, when the one who was purposed to love me, Christ Jesus was being rejected by me, the same way I was being rejected by men.

One of the greatest errors we make is giving too much of ourselves to people who will never see the value of who God created us to be in life. Today is the day to take control of your life back. Today is the day to stop the hurt of being in the cycle of death by living a dangerous sexual lifestyle. A lifestyle where at any moment you can become intimate with the person who knows they have HIV, Genital herpes, Syphilis, Trichomoniasis, Pubic Lice(crabs), Mycoplasma Genitalium, Gonorrhea, Genital warts or Chlamydia or other STD to name a few or something you can never get rid of by drugs. Today is the day you stop meeting up with strangers online. It's time to stop allowing strangers to have access to your home where you and your child resides. Its time to stop putting yourself at risk to being murdered by a social path.

Today I declare and decree that the old ways of seeking love will be removed from you. That you will seek God's face and guidance where your future mate is concerned. That you will no longer live a life of promiscuity, adultery, risking your life to satisfy your physical desires. Today I declare and decree that you be release from the strongholds of sexual addictions, pornography, lewd acts, acts against beast and nature and that you will live a life according to the design of our heavenly Father. I pray that God heal you of any and all sexually transmitted disease that you may have contracted. I bind up all lasciviousness, perversion and promiscuity and adulterous thoughts. I release the discipline, righteousness and deliverance of God of all things that are an abomination to him and cover you in the blood of Jesus in Jesus name. Amen.

CHAPTER 8
Wrongful Thinking

In the book of Exodus, it is clear on what we should and should not do as a people of God.

Exodus 20:17
Thou shalt not **covet** thy neighbour's house, thou shalt not **covet** thy neighbour's wife, nor his manservant, nor his maidservant, nor his ox, nor his ass, nor any thing that is thy neighbour's.

I had heard this scripture from my grandmother so many times when I was a little girl going to church with her and even just hanging out with her and granddad. My grandmother could quote the scriptures from one end of the bible to the other without hesitation and be accurate too.

Even though I knew this scripture and had an understanding I found myself in this place of covetousness more than once.

Just in case you are unaware of what covetous is about by definition : inordinately or wrongly desirous of wealth or possessions; greedy. 2. eagerly desirous.

It is easy to fall into the spirit of covetousness when you have desires in your life and seeing then being fulfilled in others. You began to wish you had that house or that man/woman. You think that you wish you were driving that car or you were receiving that type of attention.

There are so many levels to covetousness that we need to examine our hearts because it turns into jealousy and envy quickly.

To be honest, that is not a good look for anyone, especially a person who is walking with Christ. There is a healthy way to look at the things others possessions or spouses. You can ask God to bless you with a mate that has the Character of the person vice desiring a person's spouse. You can ask God to bless you with a home or business vice trying to take over the one that is owned and prosperous.

I had to be delivered, set free from this because I had gone against the very seed of righteousness inside of me. The holy spirit corrected me privately first and publicly. God will always use people to bring you to either a place to receive deliverance, because you have a heart of repentance and humility; or God will allow your heart to be exposed by the devil for the trap you allowed yourself to fall into because of wrongful, covetousness thinking. I have always been one of vision, of seeing myself in wealth and luxury, a world traveler.

There is nothing wrong about visualizing yourself in a wealthy place in life, where you can travel the world and buy nice houses, cars, eat and stay in 5 star /5 Diamond locations. It becomes wrong when your associates or friends are living it and you become jealous and resentful that you are not in position to do these things in your own life because of choices you made along the way.

I remind people around me who try to bring condemnation on my life(this is not of God Romans 8:1) that I am a product of the choices I have made, good, bad, and indifferent and each was used to make me and mold me into the woman I am today. I truly thank God for deliverance! I have a greater understanding of Romans 8:1 – "There is therefore now no condemnation to them which are in Christ Jesus, who walk not after the flesh, but after the spirit.

So, what changed? My way of thinking is what changed. It took me being in the heart of Somalia in 1993 for four and a half months to make me realize what was important to me. The next change was after termination of my career in the military, I had allowed the storm to change me vice allowing my faith to change the storm. The third was almost losing my child, the fourth ending a long-term relationship. As an act of rebellion against God I decided that I was not going to be active in the church because I felt I was not heard by my leader at the time. Yes people in leadership can cause you to loose heart and hope if you place your trust totally in them Psalm 118:8 It is better to trust in the Lord than to put **confidence** in man.

The word of God says: Proverbs 3:5-6

Trust in the Lord with all thine heart; and lean not unto thine own understanding. In all thy ways acknowledge him, and he shall direct thy paths.

Understand this, yes, speak to your spiritual leader. In addition to speaking to your leader, I encourage you to pray, seek God on the direction to go, he is the author and finisher of your life, he knows what is in stored for you, trust he will take you there.

People who are in the same challenge of life can't help you get deliverance. If their mind is not in a place of repentance seeking forgiveness of their sinful ways, thoughts and action. These same people will try to condemn you for wanting the change in your life and speak harshly to you about trying to be better. They will try to distract and discourage you from making the change you desire to not only have but enjoy the peace of God in your life.

Don't be so focused on how God should fix your situation that you miss out on the revelation. When you ask God to change your situation be prepared to accept "HIS WILL" not your own. I will use myself as an example. I had made my desire for relationship a god in my life, I would make my lovers first and then the church, everything else after. I thought I was in divine order because ministry does start at home first. Here is where I made relationships with a men my god-I was trying to do everything in my power to please the men I was with at the time. In my eyes he was never at fault. I was being controlled by the spirit of manipulation while I was involved with him. Especially after he was unfaithful, he took my forgiveness of his infidelity as a sign of weakness vice strength. I asked him, "What was the reason why you would step out of our relationship?". I thought it was because we were just beginning our relationship. Then I thought it was my military commitment that was causing us to be separated. I blamed myself for his inability to abstain because he had grown accustom to having to sustain a high natured woman(keeping it PG). I found myself always trying to justify the actions of men that cheated. All of it was straight lies I was telling myself. I keep getting involved with men that my dad once said as having wondering eyes, and they were constantly seeking something or someone to please their flesh.

It didn't matter what I did to please any of them I was never enough because I was not all he desired for a serious relationship. In this process, I focused more on my relationship with men who were continually stepping outside of our relationship than I was spending fasting, praying and seeking God. I was in the church doing the work, but my heart was focused on keeping up an unhealthy relationship as unequally yoked as it was with any given guy.

Then one day I got sick and tired of being alone and being in a relationship. I got sick and tired of spending my time with just me, playing and keeping house, doing the lawn, and keeping up the cars. I remember saying to myself, I am doing everything as if I am the man around here. Most of all I got sick and tired of not being respected as the woman in his life, and being neglected spiritually, emotionally by my lover.

That was a pivotal moment in time that changed my life. I repented to God and ask his forgiveness for making my relationships with the men I was with a god in my life. I began to focus on my relationship with God.

I cooked meals for who was in the house at the time. I was as a single mother, handling her own. Then, God began to do a marvelous work in me. He gave me his confidence spoken of in Ephesians 3:12 "In whom we have boldness and access with **confidence** by the faith of him."

I had confidence that my prayers were being answered and the word of God became so much alive and in operation in my life. When fear tried to come into my life, that I would not make it as a single mother, and the harsh things that was said to me out of the spirit of control, pride and manipulation, I began to profess the scriptures that God was placing in my sight and spirit. Mind you at this point in life I knew the bible, I had read it through several times, but it was when I cried out to the Lord, my savior, and said I can't live like this Please Help me Lord!

That scriptures like these began to come alive for me :

1 John 5:13-15 King James Version (KJV)
[13] These things have I written unto you that believe on the name of the Son of God; that ye may know that ye have eternal life, and that ye may believe on the name of the Son of God.
[14] And this is the confidence that we have in him, that, if we ask any thing according to his will, he heareth us:
[15] And if we know that he hear us, whatsoever we ask, we know that we have the petitions that we desired of him.

Psalm 121 King James Version (KJV)
121 I will lift mine eyes unto the hills, from whence cometh my help.
[2] My help cometh from the LORD, which made heaven and earth.
[3] He will not suffer thy foot to be moved: he that keepeth thee will not slumber.
[4] Behold, he that keepeth Israel shall neither slumber nor sleep.
[5] The LORD is thy keeper: the LORD is thy shade upon thy right hand.
[6] The sun shall not smite thee by day, nor the moon by night.
[7] The LORD shall preserve thee from all evil: he shall preserve thy soul.
[8] The LORD shall preserve thy going out and thy coming in from this time forth, and even for evermore.

Isaiah 40:30-31 King James Version (KJV)
[30] Even the youths shall faint and be weary, and the young men shall utterly fall:
[31] But they that wait upon the LORD shall renew their strength; they shall mount up with wings as eagles; they shall run, and not be weary; and they shall walk, and not faint.

I had entered a season of the wilderness of being emotionally broken and spiritually drained. During this process of transforming my mind, renewal of my mind, circumcision of my heart, God was with me; just as described in Psalms 23, he was looking out for me guiding me, comforting me with his word, through music, and even people. He was giving me moments of rest and moments of impartation into my spirit. This time of brokenness, I gave it all to God and he began a mighty work in me. Mind you, even though I was here mentally, I was still in my flesh desiring the comfort of a man too. God was trying to heal me and I was trying to find that which I finally learned only God can give me.

I tried to have the relationship I knew God had promised with me, and I went through a long period of thinking "is this him? Is he the one? Is it finally happening" to "I am sick and tired of everyone wanting relations without the relationship!". Once again, I got sick and tired of being where I was in life, I had to desire the change. The more I was in the word of God the more the desire to have things in order in my life come to be my heart's desire and in my mind. There was nothing that could satisfy my desire to have anything less than what I knew God had promised me.

How did I get there? It was a result of my prayers. I prayed a powerful, simple, I know that I am always spiritually naked before the father prayer. Meaning, God already knows everything that is and is to come, and what my mindset was already. I had to get to the place where I was willing to identify these areas that needed to be renewed and changed. By doing so, I opened the way for God to purge the old and restore the right spirit in me. I opened myself to allow God to have full reign in my life.

My prayers:

Lord Jesus Help Me!

Lord, change in me everything that is not of you! Lord purges me of all unclean ways, unclean conversations, unclean thinking, and unclean actions. I sought the Lord for deliverance from the things that was keeping me from being in true relationship with Him. As this transformation began to take place in my life, there were many naysayers, and doubters, those who wanted to whisper in my ear things like "it's not natural for you to deny your body of sex", "God understands that you are human"; "I am sure God would forgive you if you did chose to keep having sex". Yes, every one of those and even more statements was said to me from people who were in my inner circle. Trying to keep me wedged in the sin that I was seeking deliverance from, so this was my response.

I boldly proclaimed with authority "God is calling me to a higher place in Him and I must let go of things or I will be stuck. I chose to go deeper in Christ and anyone who is trying to keep me in this place will be separated from me. It is up to you to either make the changes in your conversation with me or be without me!".

I had gotten to the place where I felt that I had lost everything that would hurt me deeply. Yes, I still have my son, but I got over the fear of losing him when I was pregnant due to all the complications, I knew I had already surrendered him to Christ before birth. So, everything else, I had counted it all loss. At this pivotal point in life, I chose to live, I chose to fight for the one thing and personal relationship I knew I could not live without… Christ Jesus!

As I evaluated my life, Christ was the only person who was consistent in my life during all my ups and downs. Yes, I had friends, but at various stages, either I had violated their trust or they violated mine. So those relationships waned over time. Some of those relationships needed to end, because we had gone beyond our season in which we were destined to operate in spiritually. I say that as I reflect because I see where God brought me into a different mindset after I left the presence of negative, no hope, doubting people. People who were constantly putting death in my life situations due to the conversations I chose to believe.

I remember the winter seasons in my life. I thank God for the message I once heard that was "Don't die in your winter season". It ignited a newness in my mind, on knowing that there is hope in everything, winter is only 4 months, sometimes less depending on where you live. I smile as I am reflecting because that moment was like having smores at a campfire and no mosquitos. What do I mean by that, there is a serenity that comes with being in the heart of nature! There is beauty in enjoying simple pleasures without annoying things biting at your inner peace! God brought me to this place as I sought to get closer to him through prayer, fasting and just listening. It happened as I was singing worship songs that spoke life in my situations. All of which gave me hope to go forward. I began to live Psalms 94:18-19 KJV –"When I said, My foot slippeth; thy mercy, O Lord, held me up. In the multitude of my thoughts within me thy comforts delight my soul."

When I began to realize, I am fearfully and wonderfully made like described in Psalms 139:14, I did praise God for giving me confidence in who He has designed me to be as his child. God began to heal the years full of negative thoughts that I allowed myself to believe were true. I began to realize my beauty was not in my outer appearance but in the very depth of my heart. God was doing a mighty work in me. My mind was being renewed. I began to pray this prayer based on Romans 12:2 (my sons favorite scripture). "And be not conformed to this world: but be ye transformed by the renewing of your mind, that ye may prove what is that good, and acceptable, and perfect, will of God."

My prayer: Lord, thank you for loving me like I can never understand, Thank you Lord for touching my heart that I desire to let go of all things that separate me from you. Lord, deliver me from all sin that is keeping me from you. Please renew my mind to think the thoughts you have for me, renew my eyes to see the spiritual things you desire me to see and move upon, renew my heart to love the way you have called me to love. Lord I ask that you give me the Mind, Heart, and Love and obedience of Christ that I may walk in Godly character that I will always be pleasing to you just as Christ Jesus. Lord align my desires to the desires you have for me, align my plans to the plans you have for me that I will always be in the will that you have concerning my life. Lord bridle my tongue and control my anger, that I may be slow to speak, quick to forgive and loving in always towards your people. In Jesus name.

I ask God to bless me with the love He had for his people because I had been hurt so badly by those, I thought was for me. I like many of others have been hurt in my home, in my church, on my job and in the mist of those I called friends. Yes, every place in every area imaginable by people I would have never imagined. Yet, through it All God will get the glory because he taught me to love regardless. One day, I got this revelation about my prayer. We pray things but sometimes don't comprehend the depth of what we are asking. The more I desire to walk in the steps to be more like Christ Jesus, in his love, in his response, in my forgiving---- I had to go through the process to teach me how to do it. My pray was the talk --- the events that cause me to forgive was the walk. Many of us, yes, I mean "US" don't want to endure the pressure to be the diamond. We want the microwave version verses the home cooked meal that takes time and love to prepare.

CHAPTER 9
Torn Between Two Lovers

There was once an old song called Torn between two Lovers. In the song there was a line that went something like this: torn between two lovers feeling like a fool. I heard it one day while working in my office, and I reflected to when I was torn between two lovers.

There were many cases when I was torn by my love for God and the touch of a man in the natural. I desired to be loved and valued not for just my outer person but everything about me. Through my life's journey I was always torn because up to this point no man was willing to commit to me on that level. I had so many encounters because they were never relationships. Each encounter was only relations without the commitment… for all purposes it was a hook-up, booty call, or smashing. Whatever term you know it by, it was nothing more that sex, with no emotional connection. I had allowed myself to be used like a piece of paper that could be quickly discarded. I didn't take my time to look beyond the surface because I was caught up with my desire to be loved. I was often hidden, even in my previous marriage and so-called relationships that followed. I learned that when you are the woman in a man's life, you are on display and not hidden. A man only hides you when you are nothing more than a secret fantasy to him. The more you give to him the more he takes and it will never increase his respect for you.

I found myself torn between my desire to serve God and love him the way I desired a man to love me. Even though, I was still wanting to have a sexually intimate relationship with the man I was dating.

Noticed I said my man, not my husband. I was so far out of the will of God that I could not see the light of day. God was not having it! He is truly as the word says a jealous God. He is truly the lover of my soul, the redeemer of my life! He is my source of all things, especially my peace and joy! God loved me despite the whorish things I was doing. God loved me regardless of how often I sought in man what I could only find in Him. God loved me so much he gave me the choice to either answer the call on my life or allow him to get glory from my dying. I was not in the place where I wanted to stop living on this side of glory. So, I chose to follow Him. I chose to let go of my lustful desires I had and cry out to him with a true sincere repentive heart.

God brought me to the place where I was willing to let go of all I learned from society. The sinfulness that was the right, the in thing and delivered me from myself and my selfish desires. I had learned a long time ago that with God, I had to be all in or all out! As I learned to walk deeper in my spiritual Christian lifestyle, I live with the all or nothing mindset.

I had gotten so deep in my sinful behavior that I knew only God could change me. Especially when it came to delivering me from my sexual nature. In other words, God called me to become Celibate and I needed Him to help me stay that way! He wanted me to surrender what I loved the most sex. What was I willing to sacrifice to draw closer into him? The more I sought God for direction on my life He would reveal things and people I needed to let go from my life. The more I was obedient in letting go of the bad habits, the lustful mindset, the bitterness, the resentment, the feeling of being empty from seeking love in men who were not capable of loving me. The more I sought with a repentive spirit, humble heart the more God began to show me more of his love and reveal why those old situations were never going to work. The only man that can love me is the one God has set for me. He will love me the way he has designed to love and for me to be loved. I cried so many nights wanting to have someone to love me, to be my one true love and still being left to feel in my heart that it was never going to happen. I wondered why is the thing I desire so much the thing that alludes me the most? I was betraying my own self by not paying attention to the signs and listening to the conversation that I was having with the men who didn't want anything in their life serious they only wanted the right now.

Once I decided to be obedient and walk in the ministry of Celibacy having relationships became easier. Why, because I am sold out for Jesus! I learned the most important relationship I have ever had and will ever experience to be my relationship with Christ Jesus! Don't get me wrong, I desire to be loved and be married again, but in this season, it is NO to the sharing of "cookie", "groceries", "good", "booty", "Pum Pum" or whatever else you know sex with a woman to be called. As a close minister friend of mine once told me after a passionate kiss, "You (no one) are not worth my relationship with God. That was truly a transitional moment in my life as well. I too began to live with that perspective that no one is worth my relationship with God, and anyone who was trying to lead me to bed and not the alter had to go!

I cover you in the blood of Jesus and ask God to bridle your sexual desire until the night of your wedding. That your husband will find you as his wife, and that your wife will be found in the presence of God doing the work of His hand like Ruth in the field. I cover your thoughts and emotional responses to the opposite sex that it will never lead you to a place of temptation but to a place of revelation and elevation for God's purpose and glory as you walk closer with Him in this portion of your Journey. I declare that every sexual and emotional soul tie that is not of God be severed by the blood of Jesus Now in Jesus name forever amen.

CHAPTER 10
Just What Did I Sow?

Galatians 5:7-10 but we will focus on Verse 7 "be not deceived; God is not mocked: for whatsoever a man sowthe, that shall he also reap"

This is such a powerful scripture to remind us that all our actions in life are a seed that will return in our life in abundance. So, just what seed did I sow in my life? Lord knows that I had to pray that the seeds of deception, envy, jealousy malice, bitterness, resentment, adultery (knowingly and not knowing), bribery, blackmail, lies - just to name a few of the bad did not take root in my life. I also sowed love, time, money, encouragement, peace, mercy, grace and some material things into the life of others that I asked God to cause to multiply in my life. Let me be very clear – WHATSOEVER means just that anything we sow into another's life we receive it back even greater in ours. I reaped a lot of hardship due to my poor choices in life. I thought it was okay as a child to black mail my siblings into giving me money to keep my mouth closed about what was done when dad was at work. Our dad had the one did it you all did its mentality. So, I was going to keep quite anyway, but why not get paid in the process. I was business minded even as a child.

So, later in life, after I moved on from unsuccessful relationships, I was trying to feel good about myself. I was seeking love in all the wrong places and with the wrong people. The bible also tells us that what is done in the dark will be brought to light in Luke 8:17, I love the word of God because it is true. So, I am in the privacy of my home and with technology, I am chatting on the computer with a person. I am dealing with low self-esteem and here the poor decision was made to start sex chatting with a man on a chat. I got comfortable enough to stripe naked, what I didn't know is that this person was taking photos of me on his computer. When the conversation was not going the way, he decided it should go because I refuse to do certain things. He began to demand that I become his sex slave, I refused. Then he made the comment I would regret it one day. At the time I thought nothing of it, in my mind he didn't have proof of my nakedness. Let me tell you, satan is crafty, this man said to me "You will be famous one day! You don't even know just who you are! When you do know, I am going to uses these pictures against you or you will be my sex slave". Sounds like something out of a movie right. I wished it was, I told him, that he didn't know what he was talking about. He accused me of being bipolar because I desired a relationship but I knew he was not the person I needed to be with because bondage, domination and controlling demeanors don't work for me. I stopped communicating with this person. I found out that he was in the IT field and worked for the government. Somehow, he found out where I worked and emailed me those photos on my job. Here I was asking God, why again, but I was reaping what I sowed far greater than anything I got paid for as a child! I was so ashamed of my poor choice that I dealt with the person at arm's length until I left Texas or so I thought. When I relocated to VA, this person was able to track me, by this time I was involved with a person who specialized is cyber security and he told me how to get this person. Once again, my God made away of escape for me from that situation. I am sharing this situation with you now to encourage men and woman alike to Stop the sexting- videos that are sexually charged. You never know the intent of the person you just met. They may try to track you, sale your video or photos without your consent. This so-called discreet action could be used to cause you to lose your job. All of these are just some of the ways to bribe you into sexual favors and sexual bondage activities to show you they have control over you. It is not worth your sanity, image, name, or reputation to do such things. I ask you sincerely from my own experience respect your body, respect yourself and don't share images of yourself in sexual poses, sexually enticing lingerie, or naked it is not worth it! Especially if your relationship ends on a negative note, those images can be used to destroy your career and it is hard to prove it was not done without your consent. Even with the new laws, it is not worth it. I shared my story in hopes that others want to be as foolish as I was, this person still can post it on the web at any time, I am not ashamed of where I been because I learned a lesson. A lesson that I hope you can take and learn from without the hardship I brought on myself and my family. The lesson I learned about sexting without you having to experience this blackmail nightmare for yourself.

Other poor choices that I made was getting involved with men who told me what I wanted to hear. I got involved with men through the internet, it was the fastest way for me to meet men because I was busy with college, work and being a mom. I was still seeking to find that one man who would love me the way I deserved to be loved. Well, I was fishing in the wrong ocean. It is amazing how God will protect his children. During this season of my life, I was in a straight intentionally state of rebellion. I was angry with God. I didn't want to be in ministry, How could I preach and my life was so out of order. So, there were three things that happen that really set me on the road of practicing celibacy.

It was in the holiday season and I decided to have a sexual encounter, I found a guy I had some heated sexually charged conversations online with and we agreed that I would come to his place in another state. I got there it was snowing and when I got in the house we were talking. This guy was on the deep end of the scale of pushing the limits of a sexual experience. What am I saying this person was heavily into BDSM? What is BDSM you may ask- it is bondage consensually tying, binding or restraining a partner, for erotic pleasure. It can involve rope, cuffs, tape and other objects, usually it is a person who is dominate and a submissive person who is subjected to the bondage. It can be a form of sadomasochism. When the person met me, he said "what are you doing here?", "You know this is not what you should be doing. Do you realize you could be killed or hurt by a stranger? You need to stop getting involved with men on the internet.". I tell you; God will always give warning before destruction. Little did I know that this person was also a married person until after we had an intimate relationship.

Before I was involved in a couple of long- term relationships, I had an intimate relationship with a man that was married and I didn't know it. I asked for forgiveness and moved on. I never wanted to deal with infidelity in my relationships, I desired to always be in mutually exclusive relationships. After what I experienced in my own relationship, I didn't want to be the reason why another woman would feel that pain. Remember it does take two to be in a physical sexual relationship. Prior to my relationships beginning, I intentionally asked about the marital state of the person for the same reason, I never desired or wanted to be a side chick! I know I'm supposed to be someone's wife.

The other thing is we are never too strong to that we will not fall into the trap of our own personal lust. I had a male friend that we danced around our physical attraction for almost ten years. We had mutual military friends from our first duty assignment and was a part of the same military corps. At the time we met we were both in long standing relationships. Shortly after ending my relationship we both relocated to other locations in the states. I felt like I had dodged a bullet and not fallen into my desire to experience sexual relations with him. I was wrong, the opportunity presented itself and I blatantly sinned knowing he was married. Thinking it would be more than just good sex. I thought that we would have a special moment. It was nothing special for him, it was a notch on his belt, bedpost whatever he decided. It was nothing private about our encounter because he shared every detail with his boys and our mutual friend. One that he had already told we had been intimate years before anything ever transpired.

The Day things Shifted – well after that sexual encounter, I was driving home up I95, bopping to the music in the car and my Heavenly Father begins to speak to me. He usually likes to cut my music off and get my full attention. All I heard after the music stopped was these words

"Who do you think you are that my wrath won't touch you?" "I will get glory out of your living or your dying the choice is yours!!!".

This is the day in my life that I had reached the end of the mercy and Grace on my life. I had to make a life altering decision. It was truly a choose you this day who you will serve moment. I repented driving down the highway and ask God to purge me from all unclean ways. I also asked God to take away my desire for sex until I get remarried because I knew it was a stronghold in my life. After that moment, I never wanted to have that type of conversation with God again. I only want to hear God say Well Done thy Good and faithful servant.

I remember working a job after that and a similar situation was ongoing with one of my co-workers. I remember sharing with them, you do realize that when you knowingly are in sin, you are operation in grace and mercy, but just like any other parent, there is a time you have to accept your punishment for what you are doing that is wrong. Their reply was I just ask for forgiveness and keep going until next time. One of the greatest lessons I learned is the power in the scriptures when Christ was with the Woman at the Well. He forgave her of her sins but he expected a change to come for her and that she would sin no more. That is why I chose to live, and I ask God to keep me in my ministry of celibacy to encourage others to walk in a manner that keeps your temple holy and acceptable for the Holy Spirit to reside in you. That the peace of God may abound within you always.

I pray that this is encouraging you to get out of any adulterous relationship, any sexually immoral relationship, fornication or lasciviousness. Repent and ask God to heal you from the spirit of rejection, the spirit of promiscuity, the spirit of lasciviousness, The spirit of low self-esteem, Spirit of abandonment, spirit of molestations if you were expose to those things in your youth or as an adult.

I pray that you will surrender all that is unclean, unpleasing thoughts and ways to God right now, and ask His Holy Spirit to come and dwell in your heart and lead you to the things that are pleasing in his sight. In Jesus name.

CHAPTER 11
Generational Curses

I must make this statement clear and upfront once again, this purpose of this portion of the book is for healing and deliverance just as the rest of the book. It is not about airing dirty family laundry, a pity party or intended to bring questions or dishonor to my family or on either side, or any one's family or to those who have preceded us in death. It is written to show the importance of knowing what has happen in the past due to disobedience that is now affecting and plaguing the life of you and those before you that you just don't know why certain things are happening to you and others in your family.

I will be the first one to tell you that some of the things we don't even think too much of that are plaguing our life or our children are nothing more than generational cures that have been loosed in our bloodlines due to the acts of disobedience against God's word.

Exodus 34:7 Keeping mercy for thousands, forgiving iniquity and transgression and sin, and that will by no means clear *the guilty*; visiting the iniquity of the fathers upon the children, and upon the children's children, unto the third and to the fourth *generation*.

I know sounds like a movie right. I know that not every person reading this book believes in the supernatural or the impacts that it has in the natural realm that we live in today.

I want to discuss a few things that I have found to be the root cause of dysfunctionality within my own life. I can't point the finger at anyone and I don't care who may try to shame me for writing this chapter. In my life, I have experienced one or more of the things listed below that are considered as the root of generational curses that vexed my spirit at various junctures in life.

Deuteronomy 27:15-26 speaks of the generational curses pronounced by God, many of which we will find as the root of the outcome of many of the crimes in our society.

Some of the generational curses that vex many people in the world today is rooted deeply in the spirits of murder, idolatry, envy, jealousy, hatred, resentment, bitterness, mental health, betrayal, abortions, poverty, pornography, adultery, molestation, bribery, misleading the blind, withholding justice, dishonoring of parents, fornication, incest, molestation, witchcraft, greed, covertness, spirit of lasciviousness, lust, rape, divorce, bestiality, abandonment, jezebel and Pride spirits, drugs, alcoholism, uncontrolled anger, whoremongers, obesity, and strife.

I came from like many other people a family that could be defined as being a functional dysfunctional family. There have been seeds of discourse and comparison, and favoritism sown through the years that manifested into these generational curses that are now plaguing our spiritual walks. I am here to tell you; it is not your shame to carry! The sins of your family are not yours to bear! You have the ability to break and destroy the generational curses and cycles in your bloodline.

I remember having a conversation with a young service member here in overseas about my books and some of the topics in this book. They told me that they didn't believe in generational curses. I prepared a list of at least 100 references in the bible where it speaks of generational curses.

I was speaking about this book and how I must release somethings that will not be pleasing to some that know me. I have been told that I have no right to write this section of the book. With the boldness of a lion, I rose up and spoke to them these words, I have every right and will be totally obedient to the instructions and leading of the Holy Spirit.

The reason so many people are going through the negative experiences they are now is because of the deadly skeletons of generational curses that keep getting stronger as the generations pass. If those who first experienced it would have repented and walked in obedience we would not be impacted today.

If you reflect on conversations you have may overheard, at some point you may remember someone saying that whole family is nothing but Alcoholics, Drug addicts or whoremongers. That family is experiencing the effects of generational curses which is mentioned in the bible in several places to include Exodus 20:5, Exodus 34:7, Numbers 14:18 and

Deuteronomy 5:9 King James Version (KJV) - ⁹ Thou shalt not bow down thyself unto them, nor serve them: for I the LORD thy God am a jealous God, visiting the iniquity of the fathers upon the children unto the third and fourth generation of them that hate me,

Part of the reason why we experience uncontrolled anger and overwhelming strong urges and desires to please our flesh with the lust of our eyes against our bodies is because that seed is in our bloodline. We all have sin in our bloodlines since the fall of Adam. However, some of the curses developed because the root problem was made a god and now those are the things that plague the family. I know one of the things that is often strong in families is alcoholism. The desire for another drink became their desire to live, nothing else mattered but their next drink. There is nothing wrong with drinking, it is when you move into overindulgence is where the problems begin. Anything done in gluttony is not good.

Breaking generational curses is done by walking a life of obedience. The cure for any sin is by a heart repentance that leads to the gift we know as redemption. When we first acknowledge that there is a problem then God has the invitation to heal us in that area.

In Deuteronomy 30:19 King James Version (KJV) : ¹⁹ I call heaven and earth to record this day against you, that I have set before you life and death, blessing and cursing: therefore choose life, that both thou and thy seed may live:

We have before us life and death, blessings and curses. What we chose to serve will bring us to a spiritual life or spiritual death. What we chose to speak and worship will bring us the blessings or cursing's in our life. We have a free will. However, we must also understand that when we make choices it impacts the generations that follow us with a curse or a blessing.

It is through our faith in God that we have been redeemed. Likewise, God can deliver us from the sins of the generations before us. We as believers have the opportunity and the responsibility to receive the blessings that the previous generations didn't receive because of their disobedience.

You may be wondering why certain things influences us now the way they do. For instance, I don't drink. I don't have a desire to drink. Yet, when an intense situation happens you find yourself seeking something to calm or relax you. Next thing you know you consider the drink. Now, you find yourself having one every once and awhile. Then it turns into, I need a drink to help me sleep or relax.

I say that because that is what happened to me in my early twenties. I didn't drink nor did I have a desire to drink. I didn't like being around others that appeared to alcoholic. I didn't like how I felt when others drank too much around me and I desired never to be that person. I had a roommate who drank when we got our apartment. Every night she fixed herself a shot of liquor and drank it while she would bathe. She told me to try it and fixed me a shot of Courvoisier Cognac. I tried it while I relaxed in the hot water. Then before I realized it this became an everyday kind of thing. I went from being a non-drinker to a serious drinker in a matter a few weeks without thinking too much of it. When the Lord revealed to me what was happening, I immediately stopped drinking. It was never my desire to be a person who drank or smoked anything. I did still like wine on occasions but nothing like what I found myself getting drawn into the dependency of needing the drink to relax.

That is how simple and quick we can get drawn into the familiar spirits that linger in our family due to generational curses. If you noticed I spoke about the Holy Spirit revealing to me how I was being drawn in to the spirit of alcoholism, yet in Numbers 14:18 [18]The LORD is longsuffering, and of great mercy, forgiving iniquity and transgression, and by no means clearing the guilty, visiting the iniquity of the fathers upon the children unto the third and fourth generation.

In the book of Hose 4:6, it says plainly the reason why we as a people are experiencing such discourse and attacks within our life that seem so out of our control.

Hosea 4:6 King James Version (KJV). 6 My people are destroyed for lack of knowledge: because thou hast rejected knowledge, I will also reject thee, that thou shalt be no priest to me: seeing thou hast forgotten the law of thy God, I will also forget thy children.

I know that I was at a minimum the third generation of people in my linage that was vexed with the desire to drink and living a promiscuous lifestyle. The love of God is so great for his people that even in my wildest periods of life, God will speak to me. He will reveal to me how I was out of his will for my life. I had no clue of why I desired some of the things I did. One day I was praying after having a conversation about how dysfunctional our family seemed. Then it was revealed in the conversation about some of the things that had transpired in the previous generations. Knowledge is powerful. Learning what I did was key in the turning curses into blessings in our family. I had to make the choice to live holy or continue to live outside of the will of God. I learned to live a lifestyle of repentance.

For me a lifestyle of repentance is being in a place where I desire to be in the will of God. When He reveals things that is not pleasing Him because of my behavior or within my character, I begin to pray a prayer of release for to Him to separate me from the things that are keeping me out of His presence and will. I honestly have a heart to repent for my choice. I ask for the forgiveness and direction to go where God desires to lead me.

I can tell you about the poverty mentality, promiscuity, uncontrollable rage, manipulation, deception, hatred. These were all the things that that was destroying my life and the relationships on every level I had with the people in every area of my life. The strongholds of these generational curses had become so strong it was like a vice grip on my life.

I wanted a change and the only way the change happened in my life was because I decided that the curse stopped here! No more will this plague my family; I will not endure these things and neither will my children. God lead me to the scripture of Galatians 3:13 "Christ hath redeemed us from the curse of the law, being made a curse for us: for it is written, Cursed *is* every one that hangeth on a tree:"

We don't realize just how significant the death, burial and resurrection of Jesus Christ is sometimes. We only take it to the level of salvation, and often overlook the grace that abounds from His sacrifice of love to redeem us to the kingdom of light.

It is time to let go of the curse and walk in our new life through the cleansing blood of our redeemer. We have knowledge of how to reverse every curse, witchcraft practices and word curses spoken through the gift of repentance.

My prayer today for you is this, that the Lord will open the eyes of this person today. Reveal to them the hidden things. We are calling out to you as you instructed in Jeremiah 33:3 that you will reveal to us the great and mighty things that we don't know. Reveal to us the things that has transpired in the past that has been given legal right to operate within our bloodline. Lord, teach us the way to walk through the passage of escape for us and like your word says in Galatians 5:1, once you have freed us from the past sins, our current sins that we are not entangled with that spirit ever again. I command every demonic spirit that is wreaking havoc in my life and in our family to burn in the fire of the Holy Ghost Now. I command it to leave and never return, I shut the door on it and seal the door with the blood of Jesus. Lord, cover my eye gates, my ear gates, my front and my back gates that I will no longer use them to sin against you in Jesus name. Lord you are the strong tower that I run into and you are the keeper of my peace. Lord brittle my tongue that I do not speak things that will give the enemy legal passage in my life or my bloodline. Give me the Wisdom of Solomon, and the discipline of Christ Jesus to walk in alignment with your purpose and desire for my life this and every day. Lord I release everyone who has done me wrong. I forgive everyone who has ever wronged me and ask for forgiveness of the same of all I have wronged, from the hurt, the anger and the bitterness that it has caused. In Jesus name.

CHAPTER 12
The Transformation

Lord Help me Grow Spiritually Stronger in 28 Days

I started reading this book called Lord Help me Grow Spiritually Strong in 28 days. *It is* amazing how it worked that I never really got to finish the book, but through prayer God worked on increasing my Spiritual maturity and decreasing my flesh and carnal mindset.

I have often run into people during my journey of life. At times, God would give me the release to share my story of life. It is no different than anyone else's except that it pertains to me. It also speaks of how God has taken me through different processes – I will call them steps to Becoming.

Often, when speaking with others, I would say that I am a product of the choices that I have made good, bad or indifferent. It was those choices that molded me into the Woman I have become today. It was my spiritual foundation that has kept me from committing murder and suicide. It is my desire to please God that caused me to walk a life of Celibacy after rededication of my life to Christ Jesus and service in ministry. I praise God because of how He has delivered me from some other unhealthy choices I was about to make in life.

One thing I can say, this is not a story that is about someone who has always made the right choices. It is not about a person who has not lived the Holy life that others may profess. I am truly one that God has called out of Darkness into His marvelous light according to his word in 2 Peter 3: 9 and I refuse under any circumstance in my life to allow anyone or anything place me back into that darkness!!

In other words, God has delivered me from my past, my sins, my endiscressions, pain, hurt, confusion, frustration, unbelief and a life of promiscuity. No one has the right to cast stones and make me relive any of those dark moments. Nor do I have the right to cast the stone at those who I have asked for forgiveness and rendered forgiveness. Remember that, because God has placed you in that same position in life.

This book is intended to share the deliverance experience, at no time is it intended to focus solely on me, other than how God has moved in my life to take me from a destructive path headed to both a natural and spiritual death. Transitioning me to a life of peace and prosperity. The things that God has in stored for you are so much greater than anything you can ever desire for yourself. Let go of the desires for the material things, the possessions, the desire to be the BOSS guy or girl, let go of desiring the things that others can steal and use to cause you pain and discomfort. Focus on seeking the Face of God. Once you seek His face, God will open His hands and they will automatically reach out to embrace you as a Loving Father will his child. The blessings in his hands will be released in your life and there is no sorrow attached to them either.

One thing at a time is how you release just begin to let go. Begin to confess what it is that you want God to change. In doing so, you must understand that God's Will is not your will! You should ask God to align your will to the will He has for your life, that your desires are the desires that He has for you. Ask Him to close your eyes to all the things that are pleasing to just your eyes and not Him. Ask Him to give you the desire for the things that bring spiritual maturity in your relationship with God as your Father, Lord and King. Ask God to deliver you from man-made religions and traditions that are hindering you from having a continual growth in your spiritual relationship with him. Ask God for the love He has for His people that you will have the ability to forgive even when things happen that seem at the time so unforgivable, that you may abound in the grace of God and forgive others as you have been forgiven. In Jesus name.

CHAPTER 13
Spiritual Misfit

Hebrews 12:15 – 12:18

¹⁵ Looking diligently lest any man fail of the grace of God; lest any root of bitterness springing up trouble [you], and thereby many be defiled;

¹⁶ Lest there [be] any fornicator, or profane person, as Esau, who for one morsel of meat sold his birthright.

¹⁷ For ye know how that afterward, when he would have inherited the blessing, he was rejected: for he found no place of repentance, though he sought it carefully with tears.

¹⁸ For ye are not come unto the mount that might be touched, and that burned with fire, nor unto blackness, and darkness, and tempest,

This scripture is so profound to me because during my spiritual growth process I have been rejected by family, friends and even in the body of Christ. Rejection can bring deep scars, deep hurt that requires true deliverance from God to remove the burden that weighs you down spiritually and emotionally.

I remember when I was trying to answer the call of God on my life and the Pastor, I was under at the time didn't want me to become a minister under his leadership. I didn't really fit in because my spiritual life and convictions was more radical than the church, I was a part of at that time. I recall a candid conversation one day with that pastor about why there was no healing and deliverance in the church. I spoke up and told him that the power of God is not able to be released, that the people's faith is not stirred because they are focused on the future faith vice the now faith. I was basically an outcast because I spoke about having a kingdom mindset that comes with miracle, signs and wonders being displayed. That was not evident where I was at the time. I also spoke up about having to prime the people to worship, that worship is a lifestyle and that you can't light a fire on damp wood.

I learned something from each ministry that I have been a part of at various times in my life. Every church is called to teach and disciple the people. However, every church is not teaching on the same level. There are churches that are training grounds that release the people, there are training grounds for the babes in Christ and their ministry, and there are healing and deliverance ministries. Just as we have gifts of the spirit and each has a measure there are Christian institutions of worship that teach people at the various seasons in a believer's life.

I have been to churches where everyone seems to have it all together on the outside but then God would give revelation through prayer that there is a lot of brokenness in the body of Christ. There are people who have been classified by others who were self-haughty as spiritual cast away and misfits.

What do I mean my spiritual cast away and misfits – people that other believers and family members said would never be anything, never be saved, that their life was just a waste. Where they were rejected by how they looked and how they lived. The ones that felt like not even God could help. How wrong those thoughts are about God's ability?

The thing about the people that have been written off, cast out by men, disregarded by others, they are special to God. People don't often want to receive from other whom they don't see value in. Not the case with God, that is where God values, He puts his voice. Those that others try to make inferior God makes superior.

I been there, I been in that position. I went to a church where when I walked in for the first time, my first thought is that this is a church of misfits, all of those who had been rejected come together in one place. This is how every sinner feels when they get around people who are professing to be Christians, but those Christians only see them through the eyes the world and not the eyes or love of Christ.

That little church was so full of people of vision! People who had a heart to serve and a heart to worship God. They were a church that had a true desire to serve God's people. They had a hunger and a thirst for the presence and things of God. I remember asking God, how did I get here? God, am I a spiritual reject? Am I a misfit for the kingdom of God? I was. At this season in life, I was full of pride, I was full of hurt and I was just seeking to be healed. I wanted to be used by God for his glory, I was pleading spiritually for something to change. My presence in that church was an act of obedience. I had told God, I got to leave this dead church and where you send me, I will go just like in Isaiah 6:8.

This little church was 40 miles from my home. I went there for church, bible study and every revival. I was never a member of the church, but I was a faithful worker in the body of Christ. I needed more of God, so I pressed my way through the bad weather, the cold and even in physical discomfort to be in the house of God.

I remember one night a young 12-year-old girl walked by me the anointing of God was on her so strong, you could see the presence of God. I smiled and said how beautiful it is to have children in the Lord. I felt like I had failed my son because I didn't think I had helped him develop a relationship with God due to my past, even though he had given his life to Christ the year before. I felt like there was so much more I had to teach him. I was in a place of duress in my life, unhappy inside with myself, my job, my life and starting to feel the bondage of traditionalism in church. I was in a place where I didn't feel truly free to worship or praise God. I was having to only sing certain songs that didn't agree with my spirit. Then this young girl walks up to me and began praying over me in that revival service, the anointing of God was on her so strong! When she began praying, I was already in prayer and I felt the power of God go through my body. She began to profess that I shall live and not die and I will declare the works of the Lord.

Psalms 118:17: "I shall not die, but live, and declare the works of the LORD." That scripture began to take root in my spirit and the thoughts of depression and suicidal ideations began to leave me, the spirit of fear and failure left me too.

I began to realize that I wasn't in a place of misfits, nor was I a misfit, but I was in a place full of those who was accepted and loved by God regardless of who had rejected them. I was a person of value for the kingdom of God regardless of who didn't want to help me pursue my growth in ministry. I began to see life and people through the eyes of God. God began to show me that their hearts towards Him. He revealed the brokenness that was in me. I was there for healing of my brokenness, and the trying of my faith to trust God to lead me and guide me.

Psalm 34:18-20 King James Version (KJV)

[18] The LORD is nigh unto them that are of a broken heart; and saveth such as be of a contrite spirit.

[19] Many are the afflictions of the righteous: but the LORD delivereth him out of them all.

[20] He keepeth all his bones: not one of them is broken

God had move me to a place where I could be still long enough not to get re-hurt after my healing. God used this ministry as a rebirthing into ministry. I realized that I didn't fit in because I was called out according to

1 Peter 2 : 9 But ye are a chosen generation, a royal priesthood, a holy nation, a peculiar people; that ye should shew forth the praises **of** him who hath **called** you **out of darkness** into his marvellous light;

I never fit in nor did any of those who were there into the places of darkness that others tried to shove us into because we didn't do things according to their preference. God will always cause us to be uncomfortable when we are in the growing season. It is almost like the eagle in the egg, the time comes when we must break free from the bondages of religion, traditions and really get in the word of God to know what He says is the way to the Father. When we do, we can be nurtured, then set free to soar to the heights that God had ordained for our lives.

Often, we feel like outsiders or are made to be outsiders from those who have not learned to accept the move of God. God is now moving in the ways that are not what their previous generations have experienced. We receive condemnation from others because of their personal convictions not God's ordinances. I am here to share with you what God's word says in

Romans 8:1 -2
1 *There is* therefore now no condemnation to them which are in Christ Jesus, who walk not after the flesh, but after the Spirit.
2 For the law of the Spirit of life in Christ Jesus hath made me free from the law of sin and death.

When God is transitioning you from old ways of thinking and actions, there will be those who will try to keep you in that old dead dry place. They will try to condemn you for changing and speak as if it is a bad thing. Please, don't fall for the trap and snare of the enemy. Trust God lean not on your own understanding but speak life instead. Be like Isaiah, God where God tells you to go. Make haste and don't look back at the past and reminisce. Focus on what is ahead, look at the past as what you have overcome. Glorify God in all He is doing in your life. Praise Him for what He has delivered you from, to include people! Praise Him for where He is taking you to and that you will go with the boldness of a lion into your future. This process of being rejected, being an outcast and a misfit was truly a training ground that God allowed me to experience. So, I like you can learn not to look at the men and their faces, not to fear what man can do or will say but to walk by blind faith in the Lord. To know that the work He has started in you He is not only able but He will complete it in you! Trust God's process, it is not easy. It is necessary, it is worthwhile!

Today, I cover everyone who is reading this in the blood of Jesus, that your mind be freed from the spiritual condemnations of tradition and religious practices that have no legal bearing in the kingdom of God. That you will be released from the fear of man and his perceptions about you and your life, that you will seek God's face and wisdom. That you will now know to move and what to speak as the days go forth in your life. That you will grasp a hold and rest in the identification given to us by God in 1 Peter 2: 9 that we are a royal priesthood and a chosen generation. We are truly joint heirs in Christ, and whatsoever we ask of our Father in Jesus name that word is not going to return to us void because God is not a man that He shall lie. That you will take hold of your identity that is declared in the word of God. That by faith you will do all the miracles, signs and wonders, according to your faith. That your life will begin to go through transformation and transitional periods where God gives you deeper and clearer understanding of your purpose for his kingdom and his glory in Jesus name.

CHAPTER 14
On the Battlefield

One of my most interesting periods of life and it changed my life forever was being sent to Somalia with my unit in April of 1993. It started off as an exciting time for me because of my desire to see the world. After all the commercials referring to the people in Africa and my organization had been selected to render Humanities Aide to the people there in that part of Africa. I was excited. I was a twenty -two-year-old Soldier full of promise, pride and ideas. It is amazing how we see ourselves from the reflective place in life. I was full of the vision that my life was perfect.

Just as soon as we hit the ground in Somalia and everything changed from Humanitarian to now a conflict and my unit was given combat patches instead of humanitarian ribbons. My whole world changed too. That place taught me so much about the important things in life, it was a transitional point in my mind's eye perspective. What I mean by that is this, what I felt was important in life other than my relationships with people no longer mattered. I began to cherish and value relationship more than anything else, because I saw first-hand what happens when greed, loss of value for human life, Pride, arrogance and ignorance will cause mass destruction in a home, a life, a city, and a whole nation. Especially, if it doesn't value the life or respect of the others core values.

I quickly learned that every vow you take some are and some are not for life. It is all dependent on the individual and their personal convictions. I experienced what it was like to have thoughts of dying constantly in the forefront of the mind. I found myself wondering when it would happen. Feelings of never returning to those I love and desiring to experience the physical touch of those I loved. Knowing what it is like to become so over enticed by your emotional and flesh desires that you are willing to risk your moral values to find pleasure. Then appreciating the guidance of the Holy Spirit that brings conviction and a way of escape to keep me from making a life changing mistake. Learning the value of my relationship with God and all He had blessed me to see in life, the good, bad, joy, pain and deep sorrow.

That time set the stage for fear to wreak havoc in my life. I would go days without sleeping more than three hours for fear of what may happen in the dark. I had become fearful of dying without telling the important people in my life just how much I cared. I had a fear of being alone, if or when I was to dye in this place that was once so beautiful and now so corruptive and desolated. I began to fear, not being able to protect myself and others because of the choice's leaders made that I could not control. The only thing that keep me then and now was God.

As I returned to the states after the completion of our tour there in Somalia came a new set of fears, which grow out of the seeds that I took in while in the desert. I began to have night sweats and nightmares and would wake up alone, wondering where I was at night. My fear of being rejected, abandoned and not enough began to grow stronger each day. I began to fear that I had failed. Then I began to fear that others would know I was in a failing or they knew and thought I was stupid, blind and had no respect for myself, or desperate just to be with someone.

Here I am at home and I am on a whole new type of battlefield, my mind was continually overwhelmed with what people knew and didn't know about me. I was becoming anxious, paranoid, and began to isolate myself from everyone. Even the ones I fought so hard to get back too in my mind that I must live to see again.

It is amazing that so many people experience these same emotional battles in their minds and hearts. This ungodly fear that has been sent from the pits of hell to deter you from your destiny. The fear that is come to steal, kill and hold you in bondage of the various situations that was out of your control. While others lead you to believe it was your fault for anxiety. I took on the responsibility for things that I didn't chose, things and actions of others against me and my career. I found myself being so vexed in my spirit that I was overly alert, overly anxious. I had through fear open the door for the spirit of isolation, depression, shame, condemnation, anxiety, all followed by suicidal ideations and conspiracy thoughts.

It was during this season of personal imposed hell that God would minister to me through various songs. I would hear my dad sharing stories of his time in a hostile environment with hopes of bringing out the person I was before I deployed, the happy and joyful person. The look in my eyes was no longer one of naive and trust, but one of pain and disbelief. I was full of anger toward all that I felt had betrayed me in any way. I was angry for being put on a deployment where our humanitarian mission turned quickly to a combat zone without my personal weapon to defend me.

I was on a battlefield that was deep in my mind and it was responding and having an effect in every area of my life in a negative way.

God reminded me in his word that I was to be anxious for nothing Philippians 4:6-7 so, I had to learn to be patient with the things I didn't understand. I sought God for understanding of what was going on in my perfectly crumbled world, my career was now in question, my life had become so uncertain in a matter of months and now years.

Fear had wrecked so many of my plans, but God reconstructed my heart. God through prayer delivered me from the fear of losing what was important physically to me, what people thought of me, fear of not being accepted, rejection and shame of my past. God reminded me one day when I was crying out to him, that He didn't give me the spirit of fear. God reminded me that he had given me power, love and self-control in **2 Timothy 1:7 New International Version (NIV)** [7] For the Spirit God gave us does not make us timid, but gives us power, love and self-discipline.

God taught me through the Holy Spirit guiding me to **Psalm 141:3** ³Set a guard over my mouth, LORD; keep watch over the door of my lips. To watch the things that I was speaking. Most of my battles was what I was confessing over my life. What I was speaking was coming into my life. I learned to pray for the things that God desired me to experience, to understand the reason why somethings were not working. I sought God for the truth to always be revealed to me. That prayer strategy changed the results on my battle fields of emotions, physically and mentally.

It took years to get to this place of being victorious in my life. I had to remember that the battle is not mine but the Lords. I had to surrender it to Him to fight on my behalf. I learned when people come against me in the natural the greatest strategy is to war in the spiritual to change the dynamics of the battlefield. My power is not in the fear that was holding me in bondage. My power and my strength are found in the Lord who strengthens me and through Christ Jesus I can do all things. When I took ahold of God's word Philippians 4: 13; 4: 19, Psalms 91 and Psalms 121, I knew I could go forward. My past was not in control of me nor could fear or anyone else ever dominate me or my life. I placed my life, and my spirit in the hands of God and by faith, I have been kept through the most devastating battles of my life.

I encourage you today, to let go of the bondage of fear, it has no place in your life! Just like it had no place in mine until I gave it the legal right to be there. Whatever it is that you are fearing will or will not happen release the fear and grasp hold of your faith. For it is with Faith that we please God, it is by Faith that we receive God. By Faith we have the blessings He has ordained to be in our life. By Faith your current situation can be turned around with one phone call or contact with a person God had purposed to change your life. I say that because this is the process I went through before God could release into my life the things, He had for me. I was the hinderance to my own blessings because of fear, disbelief and lack of hope and faith in God.

When I chose to take God at his word. Remind God of his word Jeremiah 29:11-13 and Jeremiah 33:3 That He had a plan for me. I was calling out to Him to make the change. To give me the wisdom and understanding. To accept all that must happen for me to be in the position I needed to be to be used and blessed by him. I used the key that opened doors that only God himself could close.

Today, I declare and decree over you, that you will no longer be bound by the grips of fear! You will no longer live in personal hell due to fear and anxiety. That you will walk in your God given Authority in Jesus name. I declare and decree that you are restored in your confidence with the confidence of God operating in every area of your life. That the days of fearing men and their faces are over. Your understanding of your spiritual identity to walk in love and peace is upon you now. That you are a child of the highest God. That peace, love and strength of God runs in your veins. That everything that was hindering you from moving forward with the dreams and visions of God is moved out the way in Jesus name. I declare that this is the season of blessings and change and I bind up and command the spirit of Fear and all its familiar spirits to leave you NOW and return to the pits of Hell. I command every thought pattern and process that would open the door to fear to be shut and sealed with the blood of Jesus. I declare that you will experience Joy and peace of God with sweet rest the rest of your days. In Jesus name.

CHAPTER 15
Brokenness – God's beauty for Ashes

All my attempts to have a long-term relationship with the men I had dated failed. I had been chaptered (removed) from the Army. I felt I had been betrayed by everything and everyone that was dear to me. I was at a place where I questioned God and told Him that I really wanted to know what love was, I needed Him to show me what love is and how it feels to be loved unconditionally.

God began to replay my life for me in my dreams, and showed me the love of my son, the love of my Dad and those whom He placed in our lives that had nothing to gain for giving or sharing in our lives. He showed me that regardless of how rough my life may have been these two my dad and son, and a few other loved me with agape love. There are others who loved me but this was true Agape ((Ancient Greek ἀγάπη, agápē) is a Greco-Christian term referring to "love: the highest form of love, charity", and "the love of God for man and of man for God".)

My dad sacrificed himself to raise my sisters and I after his marriage to our mom failed. Regardless of what happened between them he would still remind us she was our mom and we were to love and respect her as such. My dad would give you the shirt off his back if you needed it. The beautiful thing is he would never let you know when he had given his last, He always did it in love and with words of wisdom. My dad's lifestyle became his legacy – a legacy of unconditional love. When we lost him, the love shown to our family came in so many forms. It was as if the rain from heaven was pouring out on us during that time. Dad had touch so many people in his daily walk that when we did that final roll call, there were people and Virginia Correctional officers standing along every wall with no empty spaces in between, it was truly standing room only. So many people to include myself were blessed to experience this love and beautiful soul God gave to help us through life until that day.

With my son, It was so different, we bonded from the moment I first held him, and we have been there together ever since. We have experienced many rough spots in the road along the way. Each time he looks at me it is with the love of a child and respect for his mom. My son would give anything to always ensure I never endure a hardship ever again. My son did the same thing I did to show my love and respect when all I had was just that love and me to give my dad. I became an over achiever to ensure my dad never regretted his decision to raise us. I never wanted dad to regret the sacrifice he made to give us the opportunities to be normal kids, and enjoy the finer things of life, even if it was at his own expense.

The most amazing part of all this reflection was when I began to say, I do know love. Then I felt the soft wind on my cheek and a whisper in my spirit, a little reminder that God's love is so much more than the love these two people have ever gave or can give. God loved me so much that even when I should have died in the mist of my sinfulness, He forgave me. When I chose to turn my back on Him and rebelled because I didn't get to have any real relationship as unhealthy, they had been for me. He continued to send people to show me there is so much more for me to know and experience from Him. God keep showing me the rainbows, and all I could see was the stones that was used to keep me beaten down in my spirit, feeling unwanted, unworthy, unacceptable, ugly and abused, used up and no longer valid.

One night I cried so hard out to God asking all these questions why, why no one wants to love me.... kind of deals. Then God stepped in and touched my heart and showed me why Christ died for me to know the love of his Father. That I would not live a life of damnation (the place I was while asking these questions spiritually/mentally) but a life of abundance in every area of my life. God gave me my son as a comforter, and someone to keep me stable in my decisions. I am a runner- emotionally, spiritually and physically. If I am committed to a thing, job or person, I will work to the wheels fall off to make the best of the situation. However, if I see a break point to be set free from things that are causing me to die spiritually and emotionally, just like Gal 5:1- I break camp and that thing is never to come back into my life. Once I am free of any thing that is a form of bondage, I take note and ensure, that bad relationship, that bad job, that bad church or whatever is not a part of my life every again.

I learned to love myself, even more so after I saw the movie Colored Girls. The night I saw the movie I was already in a state of severe depression, As I watched the movie, I saw myself healing from the things I had endured through the multiple characters in the movie. So much that after wards while having dinner with some associates, I wrote my longest poem ever, and my favorite to this point "Voice in the Mirror".

Voice in the Mirror

I look in the mirror and I pray to God that just
as Jabez, that I cause no one any pain
Even though my choices in life have not brought me the same
I hear the voice in my mirror as I see the reflection of me
I hear it as it seems to scream out to me. Let me be Free!
Free me from this place you have trapped me – Let me be Free!
Release me from the horrible things in your past… Let me be Free!

Let me be the substance that is now your strength
Release me from those you find as your enemy
Let go of this hurt you allowed others to dump on your life
Embrace me as the very air you breathe
Don't let bitterness reside any longer within
as it is cutting off the very life in me
Set me free from the only eyes that are yours to see
Let me be free to show the inner beauty locked deep within
Let me speak of the trails, the tribulations, the deliverance of God

Set me free in the world outside that is cold that
as others look upon you look upon me
Reflect upon your beauty locked so deeply away,
trapped beyond the pupils of your eyes
The passion that makes the heart beat loud---
the pounding of the echoes of me screaming loud ….Set me Free
As God has you to share the deliverance from the Pain

Release the Hurt- Release the shame,
let the thing I see as you look upon me ….
Set me free to go to the places that only air can flow
Let others feel what I only see each time you reflect upon me
Set me free, let me do what God has Called you to do
Allow me I beg you Set me free …. Free to Love

Why? because God was speaking to me every time I was in the mirror, telling me to let it all go! I was to love and to allow myself to be loved. Telling me to let go of the bitterness, the resentment the things that was causing me to die inside spiritually. To allow myself to be forgiven for the poor choices, to understand to listen to my spirit of discernment to go with that intuition about everything before me. That voice, I began to listen to speak to me about the heart of man toward me, to know the truth within to keep me from the bondage of fear, uncertainty and most of all depression and loneliness.

The more I got into the word of God (my bible) the more I began to shake off the ashes of the self-destructive, the suicidal person I had become. I had put all my hope and trust into mankind verses trusting in God to direct me and guide me to the place where my source of happiness and joy is always overflowing. When I look upon myself in the mirror, I would be able to see myself as the precious person God had created me to be instead of seeing myself through the eyes of man. I began to look at myself through the loving eyes of my heavenly Father. What a beautiful sight that is, to see the heart of my heavenly Father, beating so strong in me! What I love most is what God has done in my life! He is no respecter of person according to the bible. He will do the same for you if you are the person who is in this place now. God taught me when I was in this place of lack in my life that my life was not mine to take. God reminded me that it was Him that had given me life. He wanted to get glory in my living. It is a beautiful place to realize what true love is and having a heavenly Father that expresses that kind of love through His many blessing spiritually and naturally.

Lord, I pray and cover everyone who is reading this that is in a place of depression, I bind that spirit and rebuke it and the other spirits that come with its Isolation, suicidal and homicidal ideations. I bind up self-destructive behavior and lose your peace into their hearts, and mind. I rebuke and bind up every mind controlling spirit that is trying to steal their joy and peace. I declare and decree that they shall live and not die according to Psalms 118:17 to declare the works of the Lord.

CHAPTER 16
Make Me A New

The day I got to the place I needed God to make me a new was a day like no other. One of my associates and fellow poets had given me a blank book, on the cover it said, "Make Me- Mold Me" and a woman in a pink dress and a vase that was being sculpted with the hand of God. That was given to me almost 5 months before my dad passed away. Little did I know just how much that picture would be an integral part of the rest of my life to this point. As the months after my dad's passing went by, I could see how I had become that woman and that vase on that book cover.

God was strengthening me in the most challenging things in my life at that point. All my relationships were in shambles, my sisters and I were not communicating, other family members were pushing us to reconcile. There was just so much tension, all I wanted to do was just run and be on an island alone. I had felt so much pressure to be this person of strength while deep inside I was broken, hurt and lost without my dad.

I remember looking at that cover and then reflecting on who I was, who I needed to be for my son, and who most importantly who God was calling me to be. I had finally gotten to a church where I was being feed spiritually. I was becoming alive again. I was desiring to live and be a part of something bigger than my own island I desired to run to and avoid people all together.

One day after the church service, I was speaking to my Pastor's wife, the First Lady, she is such a beautiful person inside and out. I was in her office and I looked on the wall and there was that same painting. I teared up a little and shared the story with her about the blank book with the same photo. She took it off the wall and gave it to me. God has a way to remind us that we are always being perfected. We go through challenges that are the molding out our character into the image of God. Each time we chose to allow Him to guide us through our remaking and fire of our trials. On the back of that painting she wrote some words of encouragement that during new processes I can refer too in order to know I am loved and not in this alone. That the prayers of the righteous availed much.

I began to reflect and then these words came to me in my spirit and I gave birth to this poem to encourage myself as I had cried out to the Lord to Make me and mold me into the woman, he has called me to be.

Make Me- Mold Me

Lord when I asked to be made a new
to walk in the image and the mind of Christ
I never would have thought these things
That I would be hated for the peace you give me each day
The smile on my face and the joy in my heart
That it would cause so many to resent the core of my existence
I didn't realize that even those who walk in
ministry those who use your name
Would speak so much death to my spirit, not words of prophecy but
Word curses that were designed to keep me from obtaining
My spiritual destiny in you
Lord God, I never realized the true depth and extreme Christ
Truly endure for me to be free
The constant ridicule, the Judas' in his life,
The constant mission of some to cause doubt
On his true identity as your only begotten son
Lord, As you make me over a new each day
As your precious potter's hands mold this once wrenched clay
Into the Woman of God, you have called me to be-
Your Child, your minister

I know to walk in the love of Christ
Regardless of others views of who I am
When I was at my low
They talked, they scorned and they criticized
But only you Lord picked me up from my broken state
Only you loved me enough to pour your Holy Spirit
like water all over me and in me to bring me back to life
to restore me and awaken the dead, dying
and dormant gifts you placed in me
When the hate became so strong towards me
It was your loving arms I found through Psalms 91
So, each day as I arise, I plead the blood of Christ Jesus over me
The hate that was intended to hinder me has propelled me
Now as you have molded me
It causes me to love even the more
Because it is your love for me that is so Great
My Heavenly Father with each new session of sculpting
Of my murky clay flesh, you have renewed my strength
My desire and restored my focus on the Truth
Truth that there is no Greater Love than yours
For it was your son Christ that laid his life
down for mine and others like me
To redeem us from our sin and the darkness, bringing us to light
So now I comprehend when people who hate me within their heart,
The hard looks, the evil stares, the harsh targeted words and so
It is because some part of them if not all hates the light of Christ Jesus
Shining so bright within me
I realize that this hate has nothing to do with me at all
It all has to do with Christ Jesus who dwells deep within me,
In my heart and soul. It is I who has become so grateful to
be not only made but also molding in your image God!

CHAPTER 17
Worship Is greater than a song

In our day and time, it is so many things that we as a people and nation have grown to worship without even realizing it. The things that have become idols are so great it ranges from the Athletes, Cheerleaders, and Musicians, Movie stars, writers, cars, money and even Ministers of the Word of God.

Many of us have lived our life thinking that we are truly worshipping God by the things we do, but especially when we are in the church doing a praise and worship service.

One of the most profound moments in my life came when I was on a fast with a Prophet who was placed in my life for that season of growth. During our fast she turned to me and said, "Worship is more than a song"!

I began to go deeper in my prayer with God in this fast that we were in to seek God for what was meant by that statement. I am always in his presence with praise and I have a heart of thanksgiving that I express in my songs.

Then God revealed to me these scriptures, the word will speak to you when are really seeking God for revelation.

John 4:22-25

²² Ye worship ye know not what: we know what we worship: for salvation is of the Jews.

²³ But the hour cometh, and now is, when the true worshippers shall worship the Father in spirit and in truth: for the Father seeketh such to worship him.

²⁴ God [is] a Spirit: and they that worship him must worship [him] in spirit and in truth.

²⁵ The woman saith unto him, I know that Messias cometh, which is called Christ: when he is come, he will tell us all things.

We as Christians will often give lip service to God. At times, we are coming into his presence praising but we have unclean lips. What I mean by that statement is this, we just finished cursing someone out and then go into our home and begin to praise God for what he is doing. God begin to teach me that cursing was not of him.

James 3: 8-10

⁸But the tongue can no man tame; *it is* an unruly evil, full of deadly poison. **⁹Therewith bless we God, even the Father; and therewith curse we men, which are made after the similitude of God.** ¹⁰Out of the same mouth proceedeth blessing and cursing. My brethren, these things ought not so to be.

See even though I was professing things out of my mouth, they were not always what was pleasing to God, why? Because I had unforgiveness in my heart, I was full of anger, and bitterness and the fruit of my mouth didn't always align with my actions.

Matthew 12:32 - 12:35

[32] And whosoever speaketh a word against the Son of man, it shall be forgiven him: but whosoever speaketh against the Holy Ghost, it shall not be forgiven him, neither in this world, neither in the [world] to come.

[33] Either make the tree good, and his fruit good; or else make the tree corrupt, and his fruit corrupt: for the tree is known by [his] fruit.

[34] O generation of vipers, how can ye, being evil, speak good things? for out of the abundance of the heart the mouth speaketh.

[35] A good man out of the good treasure of the heart bringeth forth good things: and an evil man out of the evil treasure bringeth forth evil things.

Hearing the words, that my worship is more than a song, caused me to look deeper into my heart. I looked at the things that were keeping me from being able to get to the inner courts of praise. The things that was keeping me in bondage of fear to go deeper in the Lord. The things I needed to surrender to and repent from to shut the door to my past behavior. The things that would allow me to walk into the new thing that God was doing in my life. Mind you I am in a process of transformation in my life. When we become born again, we will be in a continual process of transition and transformation where we are being strengthened in our faith and in our spiritual walk.

Around this same time, I was invited to a ministry in Dumfries, VA, the Pastor and his beautiful wife are truly of God! I felt the love and truth of God in this ministry. The pastor had written a book called True Worshippers based on the scripture

John 4:23-24

[23] But the hour cometh, and now is, when the true worshippers shall worship the Father in spirit and in truth: for the Father seeketh such to worship him.

> [24] God [is] a Spirit: and they that worship him must worship [him] in spirit and in truth.

It is amazing how God works, because this book taught me what it meant to become a true worshipper. It taught me what is truly pleasing to God. Most importantly this book taught me how to get into His presence.

Worship requires you to praise God through your life! Praise is not just with the mouth, it done with the heart, the mind and most importantly with our spirit. We must learn to operate in the spirit of God. We must learn to let the Holy Spirit prune us of the things of the carnal mind. To cut away the things that keep our heart tied to the things of the world. We must seek the Lord our God not just for salvation, but for the guidance that will direct us to the place God has desired for us to be in life.

During this process God was stripping me from all the unclean things in my heart and mind. The more I began to press into God, the deeper I was able connect to God. I was connected to a Pastor and Wife who were not only preaching the lifestyle of worship, they were truly living it! They were instructing the people in their ministry on the ways to walk deeper into the things of God. This was a blessing and beautiful experience. It was no longer about religion or Churching it! It was about living and understanding my personal relationship with God.

I had learned to get beyond the emotional expressions of worship. God has taught me how to live a lifestyle of worship. The first decision set a domino effect into motion. It started with the decision to come out of the club. Then the decision of coming out of sexual relationships. Then it grew to a greater lifestyle consisting of fasting. My fasting lead to an increase in my prayer life. Finally, learning to pray in my holy language of tongues that I was able to experience the inner courts of knowing how to worship in truth and in my spirit. Today, I am still learning to worship in ways that pleases God. I found the key as keeping my prayer life as a staple of my spiritual life.

Even today, on my way to work, I was listening to the song "Jesus is a Love Song". It is a powerful song. It really provoked me to write this portion of the book. When we learn to worship God with the depth of our hearts and our spirit; we become willing to make sacrifices of praise. Those praises become a sweet aroma in the nostrils of our heavenly Father. When we really experience the Love of God that He has for us we try to stay in the position of being in His presence. Being in the presence of God produces a type of peace and joy that is not found any other place. When we become that true worshippers, we can transfer that peace to others. As we learn to walk in that residue anointing that remains from being in the presence of God, we can transfer that peace.

I smile because God just brought to my remembrance of how He has blessed me to walk into places and people who I had first met me will walk up and hug me. It didn't matter if it was in public parking lots, inside of businesses, or in church. The other thing that happens often total strangers will just begin to share their problems out of the blue. People who don't know God as well as those that do could sense His presence through discernment. When we live a true lifestyle of worship we become carries of God's spirit.

When we keep our temples holy and acceptable unto God, we are vessels like the arc of the covenant in the Old Testament – we hold the Spirit of God in us. That is why it is important to know God, to seek God, receive from God, receive the Love of God, and serve God by serving His people with the Love He has given you.

This is a continual process for all of us, to include me and other spiritual leaders. We are still being perfected to the image of God. That is a work that will be an ongoing process until the day Christ returns. The goal is to get to the place where we are truly worshiping God in Spirit and in truth.

Lord, we reach out to you in prayer today. Lord, I ask that you purge our hearts now. Reveal to us your spirit and reveal to us the things we shall do that will help us to get into that inner court with you. Teach us how to be the true worshippers that is able to be as your Holy Word speaks about in John 4. Lord we cry out to you like David did in the book of Psalms that you know him in always. Lord keep us from all that will keep us from being holy and acceptable to you. Lord we seek your presence, we seek your peace, we seek your love and Lord, we seek to be true worshippers in spirit and truth all the days of our life. Lord for you and you alone do we desire to worship for you are the most-high God who deserves all my praise and glory! Amen.

CHAPTER 18
Protecting The Peace in Your Life

There comes a time in your after you have sought God for his peace that you will begin to fight and sever any relationship that is costing your peace to wain or die. I can share with you how some people who felt that I had a "Nerve", "Attitude", "I think I am all that" or even the B word, when it came time for me to protect my mental peace. I will go into a little more detail to help understand what I mean.

I noted these attitudes directed at me at various times of my life. Especially during my relationships be it friendship or intimate relationship with a man after I had become a single mom prior to my rededication of my life to God. Once I decided that I am totally sold out to making Jesus famous by living a life that is led by the Holy Spirit. Knowing my purpose is to share the Gospel to all that have an ear to hear in any nation, place or area I live in. It seems like I stepped into a continual cycle of people being jealous, being critical of who I am as a person and I constantly dealt with rejection.

Through my prayer life and studying the Word of God. God led me to discover several books that dealt with the same subjects. I learned that I was dealing not with a physical battle with the people but a very real spiritual battle. A battle that had been waged against me to keep me from fulfilling my God given purpose. The battle was intended to stop the move of God in my life. If it could not stop it then certainly delay it as possibly long as it could in order to make me begin to doubt what God had revealed to me.

I had been battling against the spirit of jealously since I could remember. There were things said by our elders that made my sibling resent me and feel like I was my parent's favorite child. There were conversations that were said to my sibling and I that planted seeds of comparison, competition that became a breeding ground for resentment and bitterness amongst each other. Things were done unintentionally toward us that would cause us to question the level of love we received as being lessor than our other siblings. Yet, the truth of the matter was revealed through the revelation of God, as I sought to know the answer in prayer. Our Dad loved us all in the manner we could receive it. He gave to each of us according to our needs. In other words, there were sometimes, one of us would need financial assistance, the other would need a strong word of advice, and the other would just need to have that one on one time with Dad. Each relationship was just as special as the other. Dad was able to ensure that each one of our needs emotionally, physically and spiritually was being feed by his response to our individual need at the given time. It was only on the level that was conducive to who we were at the time in our life. I have learned that no two people are the same in everything they do in life. We can all be in the same service at Church hear the same entire message and receive a different interpretation based on our own life experience and circumstance at the time. This is the same thing that happened in our home as children. However, it took us to become adults to get that understanding. Where there once was fights amongst us to prove that we were the stronger, smarter or better one. Now it is calls of encouragement, up lifting and sharing of the word of God. God is drawing each of us closer to him. It is on us to move in the gifting and design of God's plan to use us for His Glory. Each of us are in a ministry of our own in its respective degree of anointing for the purpose God has called us to reach those in our sphere of influence.

I thank God because my siblings and I got beyond the destructive seeds that was planted in our spirits in our youth. Seeds whether planted in ignorance or not with the ultimate intent was to breed a life of confusion, competition, comparison which would lead to resentment and division for many years. I recall people telling me to be the bigger person. I stood my ground and said, No, I am not going to be the bigger person, I am going to allow God to bring it together. Because what God does when it is completed it is permeant. What man does is temporary. The hearts of those people must be in a place where they desire to have the healthy relationship with each other that God had designed for us.

One of the biggest mistakes that we do as a people is allow others to guilt us into moving in our own timing instead of moving in the appointed time of God. During this season of division between my siblings and I; I was in a deeper place of prayer and fasting. During my study of the Word of God, I came across the sons of Issachar. I ask God to give me the Issachar anointing so I would not miss His timing by trying to act on my own will. In doing so, the season of separation and division was shortened because I allowed God to work on my heart in the same manner that He was working on my siblings' hearts. The one thing about us that we learned from our dad is that regardless of what goes on in our life, when it is time to stand together as a family, we are always there for each other. I thank God for the wisdom He has given me to know how to wait on Him. How to be patient and not be in a hurry to do own my own what could only be done through God's spirit. I thank Him for healing the brokenness in my families lives and healing us all from the spirit of rejection and abandonment.

During the times where I had to make that ultimate decision on ending one of the long-term relationships I was in, one of my close friends from middle school had called me. They were able to tell that there was something not quite right with me by our conversation. I had a few weeks of high pressure from outside and inside influences. I had chosen to keep what I was going through to myself because I didn't want to be a burden. I questioned within myself how a person who had never walked in my shoes would be able to give me advice. Especially, when my decision would impact more than just my life. I had to consider the second and third order of effects of my decisions. Long of the short, I began to open and tell her what was happening and the comment from her in response was so negative, and full of "I Knew it...." kind of statements, that I just got hung up the phone. I had to shut down the "Extra" negative above the exploding emotionally volcanic mountain I was in the middle of already. When my friend pressed in and didn't give me time to cool off or to process all that I was experiencing. I did a quick assessment of my relationship with her and others in my life that were full of negativity and I immediately ended each of the relationships.

Why? How can you end a relationship or friendship that you had for over 18 years? How can you end a relationship with someone you had any amount of years of history with just like that? I ended it because the negativity was overwhelming my peace…. bottom line! I had gotten to the place where I had wanted to end my life too many times because of all the negative things going on around me. I was continually choosing to hold my peace. By doing so, I had allowed myself to be a doormat. The people around me thought they knew me to the decree that they knew what I was thinking. They had no earthly clue on who I was at all, they only knew what they wanted me to be to them. I got tired and enough was enough. Just like the emotional and physical abuse in my life, where my nights were spent crying. I had no answers. No knocks on the door from the police no calls. I got tired of sleeping in my bed alone while I was involved sexually with someone. I got tired of crying myself to sleep and being rejected by the one who was now keeping us apart. I go tired of wanting to die more than I wanted to live. Always wondering what would happen to my child if I did kill myself. Yes, I was one hot unhappy mess.

I got to that place because of these things I Identified as my errors 1) I had unrealistic expectations on others to love me exactly like I would love them 2) I gave too much access to my life to others which lead them to believe they could live my life through me 3) I didn't take heed to the Holy Spirit when I was being warned about various situations. 4) I had made an idol out of my relationships to include my friendships. 5) I had allowed my emotions to become the dominating responder in my life. I had come to the place where it was time to stop all the unhealthy pain at whatever cost. I realized that I could not give up the peace I found in my faith or personal reestablished relationship in God.

So, at this point in my life I walked away from a career, several unhealthy relationships and a few up to that point lifelong friendships. The negative impact they were all having was to much of an impact on my happiness. I decided that if I was going to do bad, I would do it on my own. I had other friends. Those who showed me that a true friend knows when to listen. When to give good godly council and when to tell me to get a grip on my emotions. Those who were bold enough to tell me to stop being a victim when God has called me to be victorious in every area of my life.

I remember sharing my joy of finally getting the courage to change the negative in my life. I was bold enough to stand up to those who I allowed to much access in my life. I made the decision to either server the relationships or change the dynamics of them. When I shared my progress with others, they took my joy out of context, So, once again I learned to be careful of what and who I shared things with. I realized that not everyone will see what I see or know how one relationship with an individual over another could have such a devastating impact on my life.

Please remember that even family members need to be given limitations on speaking into your life. I had to tell several of my family members from time to time, if all you have to say is negative, don't say anything! I also stated my relationships, my weight and my personal visions is off limits for conversation. Unless I discern that the person can accept those areas of my life and is supportive of it. Not only did I learned to protect the peace in my life. I also learn to protect the vision God gave me pertaining to my life. I began to operate in my personal life like I did in my military life. I am very strategic about who is in the inner circle. If they are not praying and interceding, they are in the boat that finds out with everyone else. People now learn about my life happenings after it is in full effect. I refuse to share in the planning stages, it is after it is in full flow. The purpose of that is to limit the distractions and naysayers trying to kill the dream. I learned that from reading Nehemiah.

The evening I told this one guy I was intimate with it was over, he laughed and said who is this N.... word that you are leaving me for?

I laughed and said you don't get it, I am not leaving you for anyone, other than the Woman that is in Me.

I learned that it doesn't matter how long you have been in someone's life, even if God brought you together. God is honoring your choice to be with someone, even if He didn't ordain them to your life because of free will. If you are not walking together in God, you will eventually outgrow each other at some point. The key is to identify that moment in time for what it is, the end of a season. From that point don't try to hold on beyond the season you were purposed. When you do hold on to long there is usually something that is said or done by one party or the other that will cause It to be a very painful separation.

The key is don't let the sun go down on your anger. It is best to end everything in a loving manner. The Word of God is true when it comes to no man knows the hour when the Lord is to return. We don't know the day when we will lose that person to death. A loss that prevents you from seeking them for forgiveness of what was said in a moment of frustrations of trying to maintain your own peace of mind and spirit. I had to learn the hard way that my happiness, peace and Joy comes from God. I must be a good steward over my peace. In the same manner I am mindful over my time and my money. I can't expect others to bring me happiness, to make me happy, because they can only enhance the level of happiness that I have already accepted in my life. One of the hardest lessons but most valuable in the same is learning to let go. I had to let go regardless of how much I loved someone. I had to learn to love them even if it was from a distance. I learned how to value my life, my peace and my joy. All of these are keys to the happiness I experience. If others could not respect me by ensuring that they were an addition vice subtracting from my happiness, then I had to let it go for my emotional and physical health.

It's Time to Invest in You

Oh, how amazing it is when you set back and reflect on your personal actions and those of others we chose to admire. The only true difference between you and that person is the level of personal investment we put into our own dreams.

What I am talking about is simply like this, I have so many books by other writers, who have inspired me. People like Maya Angelo and Langston Hughes, T.D. Jakes, Tony Evans, C.S. Lewis just to name a few. I even have motivational calendars and other works of people. I have invested my finances by purchasing and my time by reading their works. I was investing in these people's dreams. That investment is helping to make their life rich as well as mine through the thoughts they chose to share. Just as you have invested in the vision and the time that God has given me in writing this book on how He brought me to the place where I too began to see the greatness of God working in my life.

I often tell my son, "You have greatness in you because you have chosen to accept Christ Jesus, He is the Great I Am to reside in you. Because Greatness is in you, greatness must come from you!". We have what we based our faith on or the limits we impose on our self. I say that because I choose to take God at his word! In Philippians 4:13, it states, "I can do all things through Christ which strengthens me." and the scripture that says, "Is there anything too hard for God"? The answer to that question is No! There is nothing too hard for God! Nothing!

Often, we discount our own ability because we are too busy trying to compare ourselves and our abilities to others around us. This is a tool of the enemy to cause us to question what God has called and purposed us to do, It is used to impart doubt and release fear into the heart. After that is complete, we began to assonate our own vision and dream with the words we speak out of our mouths. I can tell you that stinking thinking brings negative results. For years, I have fault with weight loss and emotional distress. That was a weapon that my family and others that were around me would use to cause me pain by making it a focal point of my perceived failure. The truth was it was never the weight that bothered me. I had learned to appreciate me the way I was regardless of size, it was only when it was said as a way of causing me to feel inferior that made me feel I need to make a change, or when it was a health issue. However, those who used my weight against me used it as a means to bring shame, ridicule, unacceptance, guilt, devalued. I felt all those things, until one day, I decided to love me as I am. I am not ashamed of where I been or where I am going – I began to invest in my happiness, which required only Christ Jesus' validation. I stopped torturing myself with trying to meet the expectations of others in order to fell love, accepted or validated. I realized that was only a job for God.

One of the hardest things we as a people will do is learn to invest in ourselves the way we are so willing and quick to invest in the vision and dreams of those who walked in faith and not fear to pursue their dreams. We have the same opportunity to be our greatest asset or our worst liability through the things we think of ourselves. What happens to us is never a reflection of those around us. It is about how we chose to respond to the environment we allow ourselves to be a part of that will either birth or kill our vision.

God has given us a measure of faith, and His Grace is enough for us in all we endure. We just need to trust and believe. That vision that He has given you, pursue it! Begin to put your confidence in the Lord, and less in people. Pray and ask God to bring the right people in your life. Those who are purposed for His glory in your life. That you will always be aligned with God's will and purpose. That as you begin to walk in the birth right, we have as joint heirs in Christ Jesus, we also have the confidence in God that He is always with us according to Psalms 27 and Psalms 23. The key is this- we must seek the source of our strength, the source of our love, joy, and peace.

The circumstances in my life changed so drastically, that I had two choices, I could have given into all the pain and hurt of my past and commit suicide or chose to live. Choosing to live required that I would have to step out on faith. I would have to trust that God was able to heal me of the pain. He could give me the desire to love again. He was going take me from the lowest point in my life and take me to a place only He would get the glory from me and others. Instead of staying in the pain, I chose to live and pursue my dreams.

I must be totally honest with you, getting higher education was not my desire. However, because of necessity it became something I had to pursued in order to give my son a better way of life I needed higher education to earn money to stand on my own. I am sure at some point in time you found yourself doing things more out of necessity than desire to ensure that either you or those you care for had the best in life. I didn't want to pay the cost to get the education. I felt that I could invest that money better in other ways. Yet, the degree was required to meet the need to care for my child. I stepped out on faith and began college in 2000. Because of my choice to join the military after high school, I had funds in the GI Bill to help with college bills. The blessing was how God provided a way that my education up to part of my first master's degree was paid for through that one choice. I spoke on that to share this point- a choice you make today may seem insignificant. That same choice can have a major blessing that is time released in your future that will bring blessings you beyond your imagination. I am a living witness to that my blessing have been in abundance. When I chose to step out on faith and trust God to make a way for me to be the best mom, employee and student I could be, but especially becoming a child of God, He did just that for me!

My process to the best life I could imagine for my family and I began when I decided to apply the kingdom principles to my life. First I began to seek God for his guidance, His will and way for me in accordance with Luke 12:31. Then I put my trust in God that the things He had started in me or allowed me to begin He would also allow me to complete it.

I had begun to walk in the promise of Philippians 1:6. I had to sincerely trust the Lord with all the challenges and changes, and just know that His plan was better than the plan I had for myself. This was tied to Jeremiah 29:11-13, and Proverbs 3:5. The thing I learn the most from conversations with my dad was the bible truly had an encouraging word for every situation that I was encountering. I just had to apply it to my life for my peace to come.

Today, I pray that just as God is not a respecter of persons, that the same overcoming anointing and grace that He placed on my life, that you will be like Timothy and run the race to the end. I pray that you will fight the good fight and be found a strong soldier in the kingdom of God. That you will not grow weary in the low points but that you will always cry out to the Lord Jesus Christ and know that according to Psalms 121 and Psalms 91 that your help is from the Lord and He will protect you as long as you abide in him.

Prayer and fasting were key to my strength. There will be seasons when your faith will try to wan but that is when you need to spend more time in God's presence through prayer, worship and praising him for all that He is allowing to happen and all that he prevented as well. When you truly reflect on your life, I am sure just as I have you will see points in time, where you must be grateful for what you desired and God did not allow. You can see now that it would have been detrimental to your personal and spiritual growth. So today, I challenge you to do the unthinkable, what seems impossible, step out on faith and invest in your relationship with God. Invest in the visions He is birthing in you. Watch the transition from grace to grace, mercy to mercy, and from glory to glory take place in your life. Knowing that your life will be enriched in more ways than one. It's time to experience the abundant life in Christ Jesus, your choice will either bring it to pass or delay it from starting.

CHAPTER 19
Beautiful but Deadly

After our deliverance process, we have some people in our lives who have a very low impression of who were are in life. These are people who too have allowed God to complete a mighty work in their lives. Yet, somehow, these people cannot see the mighty work God has done in delivering you because they choose to try to keep you in the place called Lo-debar (no word or "no thing") mentioned in 2 Samuel 9.

They desire to keep you in that low place where they think so little of our God, the Father of Christ that He is unable to move in your life the same way He moved in theirs to free them from sin. It is amazing how some people will never see beyond the sin you use to do in order see the greatness God is working in you now.

When I am approached with those type of people now. I limit my interaction. I have learned to keep at a distance. My response when the conversation begins with the sins of my past, You know "That is why I thank God for DELIVERANCE!!!!"

Yes, that happens to you. It just reminds me of the Word of God in Romans 12:3, that we should not think more highly of ourselves…. I Thank God I am no longer in that place.

God revealed to me the truth of those moments as being spiritual attaches. What was really happening in this situation is the individual is either knowingly/unknowingly allowing themselves to be used by the devil in a spiritual attack against you.

See the devil will always speak to the sinful nature you were in, bring up all the things that was not of God as if it is still enjoyable and pleasing to you. If you noticed each time the attack came, it was combated with the acts of Faith, the acceptance of my new Identity in Christ.

I can boldly proclaim that I am saved, I am delivered from my past, I no longer am I a fornicator, adulterous person, backsliding, cursing, evil scheming, jealous, gossiping, uncontrolled anger, abused, abusive, neglected, abandoned, betrayed and unforgiving person, that is the short list, just so you can get the point.

You know that you too can go down the list that God has delivered you from, starts speaking in with a simple prayer or praise of Thanksgiving to our heavenly Father. I do it all the time when I am driving.

There is a song I use to sing, and it would get me to shouting in the Holy Spirit because I am so grateful for where God has brought me. The song says, "When I think about Jesus and all he has done for me, when I think about Jesus and how he set me free, I dance, dance, dance all night!! I don't know about you but I have joy unspeakable in my life. Just like in

1 Peter 1:7-9 (KJV)

7 That the trial of your faith, being much more precious than of gold that perisheth, though it be tried with fire, might be found unto praise and honour and glory at the appearing of Jesus Christ:
8 Whom having not seen, ye love; in whom, though now ye see him not, yet believing, ye rejoice with joy unspeakable and full of glory:
9 Receiving the end of your faith, even the salvation of your souls.

I have truly been tried by the fire! I know that God is still taking me through some refining processes even at this stage in life. Living a life sold out to Jesus, is a journey full of growth and progression, it is all according to our faith in God's ability to move like He said He would move.

Often, as I spoke of earlier, we limit God's ability to move in our life because we get stuck in the lies that others try to impose on us. We then believe that we are so deep in our sin that we are unable to come out of that dark hole. However, we must take hold to if nothing else these few scriptures;

First : Is anything too Hard for God?

Jeremiah 32:26-27 (KJV)

26 Then came the word of the Lord unto Jeremiah, saying,
27 Behold, I am the Lord, the God of all flesh:
is there anything too hard for me?

Second: understand you new identity in Christ

1 Peter 2 (KJV)

1 Wherefore laying aside all malice, and all guile, and hypocrisies, and envies, and all evil speaking,
2 As newborn babes, desire the sincere milk
of the word, that ye may grow
thereby:
3 If so be ye have tasted that the Lord is gracious.
4 To whom coming, as unto a living stone,
disallowed indeed of men, but
chosen of God, and precious,
5 Ye also, as lively stones, are built up a spiritual house, an holy priesthood, to offer up spiritual sacrifices, acceptable to God by Jesus
Christ.
6 Wherefore also it is contained in the
scripture, Behold, I lay in Sion a
chief corner stone, elect, precious: and he
that believeth on him shall not

be confounded.
7 Unto you therefore which believe he is
precious: but unto them which be
disobedient, the stone which the builders
disallowed, the same is made the
head of the corner,
8 And a stone of stumbling, and a rock of
offence, even to them which
stumble at the word, being disobedient:
whereunto also they were appointed.
9 But ye are a chosen generation, a royal priesthood, an holy nation, a peculiar people; that ye should shew forth the praises of him who hath called you out of darkness into his marvelous light;
10 Which in time past were not a people,
but are now the people of God:
which had not obtained mercy, but now have obtained mercy.
11 Dearly beloved, I beseech you as strangers
and pilgrims, abstain from
fleshly lusts, which war against the soul;
12 Having your conversation honest among
the Gentiles: that, whereas they
speak against you as evildoers, they may by
your good works, which they
shall behold, glorify God in the day of visitation.

3) Walk in your new Life and Identity in Christ Jesus according to

Galatians 5: 1 (KJV)

Stand fast therefore in the liberty wherewith Christ hath made us free, and be not entangled again with the yoke of bondage.

So, let's take a minute to really look at Galatians 5:1, this is so powerful!! God uses this to minister to me when I am getting drawn back to a place that He has already delivered me from through faith. The thing is that we can go backwards through a subtle process of compromise in our actions. We get drawn in by the familiarity of the thing we were apart of previously.

How do we compromise? When we entertain comments or make confessions out of our own mouths things such as this "oh, I am sure God would not mind if you did it just this once", "God knows you are human, and sex is a natural process of life", "it won't hurt you to go to the club, have one drink ",

"Who's going to know you did it other than us".... I am sure someone is saying Man, that does happen. I know, because each one of these things has either fell out of my mouth or someone else's to me. The closer I was drawing to Christ Jesus the more He was shutting down the connections I had to my sin.

The word of God says, in Luke 12:48 (KJV)

But he that knew not, and did commit things worthy of stripes, shall be beaten with few stripes. For unto whomsoever much is given, of him shall be much required: and to whom men have committed much, of him they will ask the more.

We have been given so much in the way of our mercy and grace, that we have eternal life. What is required is to walk in our identity as a Royal priest hood, Child of God (from his spirit), Joint Heir in Christ, operating in the Holy Spirit, and displaying the fruit of the spirit in

Galatians 5 : 16- 26

16 This I say then, Walk in the Spirit, and ye shall not fulfil the lust of the flesh.
17 For the flesh lusteth against the Spirit, and the Spirit against the flesh: and these are contrary the one to the
other: so that ye cannot do the
things that ye would.
18 But if ye be led of the Spirit, ye are not under the law.
19 Now the works of the flesh are manifest,
which are these; Adultery,
fornication, uncleanness, lasciviousness,
20 Idolatry, witchcraft, hatred, variance, emulations, wrath, strife,
seditions, heresies,

> 21 Envyings, murders, drunkenness, revellings, and such like: of the which I tell you before, as I have also told you in time past, that they which do such things shall not inherit the kingdom of God.
> 22 But the fruit of the Spirit is love, joy, peace, longsuffering, gentleness, goodness, faith,
> 23 Meekness, temperance: against such there is no law.
> 24 And they that are Christ's have crucified the flesh with the affections and lusts.
> 25 If we live in the Spirit, let us also walk in the Spirit.
> 26 Let us not be desirous of vain glory, provoking one another, envying one another.

We do not ever have to compete against anyone to get God's attention! He is focused on each of us and our individual relationship with Him. He looks at how we treat others as an expression of His love through us. That one is profound! If you have children you know that you want them to "represent you" well, meaning when they are out, they are living a life that is Godly, and wholesome.

God is our heavenly father, and here on earth he desires that we walk in the world, but not be of the world.

> Romans 12:2 (KJV) 2 And be not conformed to this world: but be ye transformed by the renewing of your mind, that ye may prove what is that good, and acceptable, and perfect, will of God.

What does this really mean? We are to enjoy this life, have fun, laugh, be prosperous and in good health. It also means that we should keep ourselves holy and acceptable to God. We do that through obedience to the guiding and direction of the Holy Spirit, not allowing any and everything to enter into our eye gates ear gates, front and back gates (private areas) mouth gate.

So, watching pornography feeds the spirit of lust, listening to cursing and anger provoking comments leads to discourse. Knowing what your food source is and how it's purpose before preparation is important. Especially, in foreign countries during various festivals. If you are unsure if what you are eating was used as a sacrificial offering to a pagan god before you were served it? Then don't eat at the festivals.

Most people don't think about that one. I learned more about this as God opened the door of opportunity for me to travel throughout the world. He began to expose me to various cultures, allowing me to watch their festivals or even those who participated in them.

Before I decided to participate in any of the seemly harmless events, I chose to research, knowing the deeper meaning of things is so important and keeps you out of unnecessary spiritual warfare. People unknowingly invite spirits in by the idols being brought into homes by not understanding the intended purpose of the item.

Lack of knowledge is not a beautiful thing at all it is deadly to your spiritual walk. God began a process of gaining deeper knowledge and wisdom in me through the art of researching things. Knowing the why, where and how things evolved, like Yoga, Hinduism, Buddhism, Tao, Muslim faiths and various countries cultural practices opened my eyes to the way we allow other gods, and spirits to enter our homes. We open a portal for them to operate legally and gives them right to vex our spirits.

I had the pleasure of living in Japan for a while and what I found so beautiful from the outside looking in was the upkeep of traditional dress, beliefs and practices. I wanted to know what are all those Pi gateway looking things and what is their purpose.

God started dealing with my heart to research. During this time, He was reminding me that everything that is beautiful is not always good for you. Torii gates are traditional Japanese gateways most commonly found at the entrance of or within a Shinto shrine.

Torii gates symbolically mark the transition from the profane to the sacred. One of the local nationals in Japan explained that it allows the spirits of their ancestors to come and go between the spirit and natural worlds.

The purpose is to mark the entrance of a sacred space. There are ways to distinguish between a Shinto shrine (sandō) which is almost always straddled by one or more torii. The outer torii is called ichi no tori and the ones closer to the shrine are called in the order you approach ni no torii and san no torii.

There are other torri further into the shrine that is used to represent the increasing levels of holiness as, one nears the inner sanctuary (honden) or the core of the shrine. The Japanese Buddhist temples have their torii gate standing at the entrance of the temple's own shrine, and it is called chinjusha and are normally very small structures.

So, looking at the intended purpose of the object it is to allow spirits of the ancestors or gods to freely move in and out in their cities, homes, and lives.

When I was in Africa, I learned about the traditional African mask, some are used in ritual and ceremonial events, most of the mask usually have a spiritual and religious meaning they were created for as well. Among the traditional African cultures, anyone who wears a ritual mask takes on the spirit that is represented by the mask and loses their human identity.

There are other practices involved in this transformational process, which may include music, dance and other ritual costumes that will reinforce the spiritual identity while concealing the human identity. In these instances, the person wearing the mask acts as a medium that is a conduit for a dialogue between the community and the spirits which are usually dead or nature related spirits.

These rituals are found in their wedding, funerals and initiation rites throughout various tribes. The University of Virginia has references in "The art of African Mask" which breaks down the faces of the spirit.

We must guard the spirits that are attached to items and articles we bring into our homes that change the atmosphere because of the spirits they carry, because of their intended religious use.

People how practice some forms of yoga get into the practice of Levitation. Levitation is the phenomenon of psychokinesis, which is the act of objects, people or animals rise in the air without visible physical means, which allows them to float or fly about. This is usually the result of demonic possessions through acting as a mediumship, shamanism and trances.

We must be careful that we do not study or practice things that allows demonic spirits to come into our spirit because we are opening portals for them to operate in our life.

The word of God tells us :

> Hosea 4:6 My people are destroyed for lack of
> knowledge: because thou hast rejected
> knowledge, I will also reject thee,
> that thou shalt be no priest to me: seeing
> thou hast forgotten the law of
> thy God, I will also forget thy children.

It is so easy to get involved in things that look easy, like it is a simple dance, a beautiful piece of Art, or just a form of relaxation. Know the origin of the things that draws your attention. Some of the most beautiful flowers and creatures have the deadliest venom.

It is our duty and responsibility to keep not only ourselves aware of the things that are in our presence, to seek discernment of the spiritual nature of people and objects and keep those we know aware of the same knowledge.

My prayer for you today is that you will never lack again in knowledge of the hidden deadly beauty that the enemy has sent to distract you from your purpose. That you will have a quickening in your spirit that will expose everything that is sent to trap you and distract you, that is sent to curse you. I declare and decree that you will take authority over every ungodly thing and cast it down and remove yourself from it and those who are trying to draw you away from your relationship with God. In Jesus name.

CHAPTER 20
A moment of Influence

A profound moment of influence.

I love how God will set the stage for you even when you are desiring to stay behind the scenes. I recall being in a training group for a leadership program. The method of teaching was a little different than what we all had been accustom too. I like to observe the situations. I have found that I learn more by listening to others than always trying to be the one speaking. I am often mistaken by others as not having any relevance.

However, I learned early in life if you are always talking then people will get tired of hearing what you are speaking. They will want to know something new. This training day, we were asked a series of questions and we had to prove our points.

The question was Does faith exist? If so, prove it! Many of my classmates who like me had a spiritual relationship with God began to answer the question. Much to all of our surprise when they use the argument of the Bible or other religious statements they were told to set down.

I found that with each one of them been refuted, that the spirit man in me began to become more angered. However, I remained calm, I boldly raised my hand to go before our instructor and defend Faith. After all, everything in my life is in existence now because of my faith.

Prior to the moment of me raising my hand, God brought back to my remembrance the day that I was walking and I was admiring all His creations. I asked God the question, Lord, how is it that people are denying you, when there is so much proof of who you are in everything created.

I heard in my spirit that for them to deny me, means that they acknowledge me therefore they can't deny me.

So, the instructor calls on me and says "Does faith exist? I responded yes; Faith does exist. He smiled and said prove it. I then boldly responded with the answer I received years ago,

"For you to question Faith's existence means that you acknowledged it, therefore Faith exist." I stood there waiting. There was a long moment of silence that fell over the room, and then the instructor walked away and sent us on break.

The next night was the same questions were asked again. However, someone else answered the question, they tried to remember what I said the night before but didn't' get it right and was told to sat down.

It was at that moment that God showed me how subtle but quickly He has caused me to impact a person or a group of people with the wisdom He has given me.

I said that for this one purpose. Don't stop speaking up when your spirit is telling you to release a word. There are things that may seem so odd, or unmeaningful to you but it will be the water needed in someone's desert seasonal that those words will bring life back to them.

It is amazing how our words will not only influence our outlook but the outlook of others. I remember not being comfortable with speaking in public or around others because I felt others thought I was stupid when they would respond to my comments in a negative way.

I later learned by the teaching of the Holy Spirit that others would try to discourage me and put me down because of the depth and profound thought that was in my conversation. There are people who is sent to build us up and there are those who are on assignment to tear us down, to keep us in a low place.

It is vital to our spiritual walk that we do as we have been instructed in Jeremiah 33:3 and James 1:5, If we are lacking wisdom we need to cry out to God and ask Him for the wisdom and allow Him to show us the things we don't know.

My prayer for you today is that God will reveal to you the spiritual and natural influencer he has created you to be. That God will give you greater wisdom, and knowledge of the things concerning your area of specialization, that those that you are called to influence will see the beacon of Light of the Holy Spirit within you and uses you to help mold the next generation of influencers in your community, nation, region that you may strengthen, encourage and impact your territory with other believers, that are called to do great and mighty things through Christ Jesus.

CHAPTER 21
Hurt to The Core

I will begin this section with **Psalms 147:3 He healeth the broken in heart, and bindeth up their wounds**. One of the things I know for sure is this, we all have experienced some form of painful event that hurt us to the core of our very existence. Something that experience was so unreal, unexplainable, unsolicited, unwarranted, undesired and most of all undeniable.

I spoke about a few of these types of events that have happened in my life already. A few years after my one of my long relationships ended, I relocated to northern Virginia. One morning while I was at work doing my normal mail run, I encountered a co-worker who was so devastated that she could hardly talk. I asked her what was wrong. I was expecting to hear the loss of a loved one or loss of a pet from the way she was crying. Then she said, you wouldn't understand now one can understand where I am right now. I told her, that may be true but I am here to listen as a friend if it will help. We walked outside and then she shared her story.

When she finished, I told her I truly understand where you are right now. I know the pain that is in the core of your existence. I know every thought that has truly ran through your mind. She looked at me with shock and I smiled. I told her you have two choices you can be angry, hurt, bitter and resentful or you can forgive and move forward with your life with or without your husband.

She looked at me with confusion, I went back to my office and I typed up how she was feeling on a blank piece of paper. What I was really doing was releasing the hurt of my past in order to help someone else who was in the same place I once was to heal. I went back over to her office and gave her the poem and said to her "is this how you feel?" She looked at me with a sense of relief in her eyes, that someone did know what she was going through right then. She had discovered a newfound peace in the mist of her chaos. I shared my testimony of the day I was hurt to the core with her. The poem is called It Hurt Me to the Core.

It Hurt Me to the Core

It hurt me to the core of my very being. The pain was worse than ripping my heart right out of me, you the man I love the one I trusted, the one I invested all my time, all these years.

It hurt me to the core of my mere existence, this pain. I don't understand why or how you felt I need not know about the child you had, yet you robed me of that dream. The joy of being a mother having one of my own. As you told me we were enough for one another.

How could you be so casual, so nonchalant about this situation? As if it was a mere payment on a loan you had! This is a Child, even though not mine, a part of you. You took away my choice! To accept to be angry, all you left me with is pain and betrayal.

Yes, it hurt me to the core! My body is in total shock; my heart no longer desires to beat. Everything I knew as truth is all tainted with lies. I wonder, how you felt, each time you seen a child? Knowing you had one, knowing you denied me of one. How could you be so bold as to lie to me over and over again?

Did you enjoy the pain it brought me? Did you think it would make me still want you? Did you realize I was not as weak as you had determined? For today, I told you I desire you no more. Today, I saw my lawyer. I no longer will be hurt to my core by the one that I once adored.

The healing begins from the inside out, the core of me, is not rotten by the lies, and deceit you brought in. It is rejuvenated by the love I hold I me! Knowing me, loving me! So, I refuse to hurt anymore, especially in my core.

As you think over the past, you too may have experienced events I am sure that just like this one impacted you to the core of who you are as well. You know what it is to live in a place in time where it shattered your world and devastated all you believed to be true in your heart.

Yet, there was something inside of you that pushed you to believe and know that you deserved so much more than you were experiencing. Something that reminded you his is not what God has for you or ever intended for you to have to endure. However, you are there, enduring and overcoming the tears, the pain, the fears and disbelief.

When I was crying out to the Lord, He reminded me of His word in Psalms 34:18 "The Lord is near to the brokenhearted and saves those who are crushed in spirit". Yes, my spirit was crushed, my soul seemed to be crushed I felt like I had been hit with a Mack truck and ran over to ensure I was not alive. Yet, I was still existing. I went from being a person full of hope and love to one that was filled with bitterness.

In that time of praying and yelling at God to be totally honest. He reminded me of a couple of things one that He is a jealous God, there will be no other gods before him. I had made this particular relationship at this time a god in my life. The hidden things that were done in the dark was being revealed to me and I could not deny them.

If letting go of all I thought my future would be was not hard enough. I knew I had to give up my dreams of this relationship being a lasting one too. As God was transiting me to understand what he was meaning in Psalms 51:17 tells us "The sacrifices of God are a broken spirit; a broken and a contrite heart, O God, You will not despise." As much as I was hurting to the depth of my being, I had to forgive and I had to continue to love.

I experience more hurt and betrayal by those I thought had my best interest at heart during my early adult years. I experienced spiritual hurt by leaders in the church who were supposed to pray with me who were talking down on me because of how I chose to go through my process of letting go.

I was accused of being less than a woman because I had been physically abused. I was treated like I had never received the Holy Spirit. I was treated like I could not be used by God because of jealousy, envy and resentment because of how God chose to use me. I was accused of trying to lead people to sin because of leaders trying to project their character on me. My character has been questioned, my call has been questioned, the anointing has been questioned. Each time the direction of the attacks and the way it came was not always with love but that sharp double edge sword and words that cut deep.

I know others can relate to some if not this chapter in its entirety. However, God reminded me of these things. God reminded me that I was His minister, in public and in private settings. People tried to make me not believe that I was called. God reminded me of Matthew 22:14 "For many are called, but few are chosen" and Philippians 1:6 KJV Being confident of this very thing, that he which hath begun a good work in you will perform *it* until the day of Jesus Christ:

God made it publicly known one night in a church service. I was hurting so bad to the point of being emotionally suffocated. I felt if I didn't get to the church to pray with the power of agreement that I was going to die. It was that night during the bible study that God revealed to that small congregation and to reiterate to me who I was in him. I was told not only am I His minister, but I am His Chosen, and it was time to be about my Fathers business. God had not only put His seal, He also put His mark on me!!

As the attacks on my character came after I had rededicated my life to Christ, I remember asking God the question of how can those who are so deep in you in prayer not able to see the transformation in me. I was hurt so deeply by an associate in ministry who I felt was a person God had purposed to help me draw closer that I wrote this poem out of my pain.

The Best In Me

God how is it that you see the Best in Me? The Soul who
has been cleansed with the blood of your son Jesus, the
child who is now pure and transparent to your eyes.
God how is it that you see the very best in me,
the own you had called out of darkness
The one you have saved from sin, sexual desire
The one you kept from being murdered, from suicide
The one you delivered from abuse, neglect, strive and envy
You see me as one you have Chosen to do your work
Yet those who are also your children, whom you have done the same
For whose sin you removed choose to see the very worst in me.
How is it that you have done the same for them, yet it seems
impossible for you to have cleansed me and deliver my soul?
God how is it possible for you to see the Best in me
and your children still try to deny what you have done for me?

One thing I have learned in this life when you are trying to find the peace and live a simple life for God, doing His will, there will always come opposition to your existence. There will be people who will never accept the change God is doing in your life, or the choice you made that has allowed God to move greatly in your life.

God reminds me often of Jeremiah 1:8 "Do not be afraid of them, for I am with you and will rescue you ", declares the Lord. In other words, this is what I need for you take to heart. No matter who or what comes against you, God will come to your rescue. God will heal you of every deep cutting word that has wounded you spiritually and emotionally. God will heal you of all the stabs at your character and your integrity as you walk with him. Then God will reveal that all the attacks against you is really to discourage you from reaching your spiritual destiny. They are sent to kill your purpose, to kill your trust, your peace and your joy in the Lord.

I pray that you who has either experienced this in the past or is currently going through this process will hold on tighter to your confessions of faith, Remain in the hands of God according to Psalms 91 and let His protection shower your mind and that you will walk in the confidence in the Lord according to Psalms 118:8 "It is better to trust in the LORD than to put confidence in man." Man will try to take glory for all that God is doing in your life and when you are being accelerated in your purpose God will redeem the time that has been lost. The enemy will use any and every one to try and distract you from what God is revealing to you. The enemy will try to keep your focus on the distractions in order to blind you to the promises and purpose of your call.

I pray for every person who is hurting emotionally, physically, spiritually, that you will surrender that pain to the Lord and allow him to restore your joy. God's word in

Isaiah 61:3 - To appoint unto them that mourn in Zion, to give unto them beauty for ashes, the oil of joy for mourning, the garment of praise for the spirit of heaviness; that they might be called trees of righteousness, the planting of the LORD, that he might be glorified.

God wants to restore your peace, your joy, your praise and remove all the spirit of heaviness that has come in your life, remove all the spirit of doubt, inadequacy, weariness that has tried to plague your heart and spirit, that is trying to take control of your mind and keep you in a desolate and cold place. The Joy of the Lord is your strength and I command every spirit of dissolution and traps of the enemy to be exposed. I declare and decree that the pain and bondage of pain of word curses, acts of betrayal physically, mentally, emotionally no longer control your mind, that they are erased as far from you as your sins have been removed. I release the peace of God to rest in your mind and spirit that even when you come across those who have offended you in the past. That you will extend the love of God through forgiveness and asking for forgiveness as well that you will be set free from the bondage of forgiveness so that you may also be forgiven by the Father, the author and finisher of your faith. The one who has not only called you to purpose but who has also equipped you through the Holy Spirit to complete the work that He has started in you. That you will have a zeal and a passion for the work of God that will cause others to want to know your God and serve Him too. In Jesus name.

CHAPTER 22
God's Uncommon Way for Me

It is amazing how God decides to do things in our life that will do two things for sure 1) ensures no one can take his glory and 2) make everyone know it is only God. I can truly say that for my life especially when it comes to the ministry.

I started in ministry at a young age. I was with my grandmother in my youth, when she would go clean the church my sister and I would go with her. Yes, cleaning the church is a form of ministry and it speaks to the heart of the person. I learned early that when you are faithful over the few things God makes you ruler over many. It is also God who promotes not man. Man can never validate who God has called nor will they be able to stake claim on the birth of the ministry within a person, even though there are many leaders that try.

When I first really accepted the call on my life, God gave it to me in a vision at the age of fourteen. It was such a rich vision that it spoke about healing, deliverance, prayer, and casting out demons. The key to that vision was God had shown me that He had equipped me for battle. I would be successful at battle. However, I had to ensure that I had on the whole Amour of God spoken of in Ephesians 6. The vision was so powerful because it showed me that God would walk with me and instruct me in the things I should go as well according to Psalms 32:8. God let me know that He had called me to do mighty things, but I got afraid. I began to run, and I was running from my destiny and I was running to death, naturally and spiritually.

I found that in my running, I was trying to connect with everything that I felt would make me less desirable for God to use. I was having a Jonah moment. During this season of rebellion and running from destiny God would use strangers and people I just met to speak into my life and tell me things like, Matthew 22:14 "Many Are called but few are chosen". They would tell me to" be strong and of good courage "Deuteronomy 31:6. And the one that always got me was the 1 Corinthians 2:9 "But as it is written, Eye hath not seen, nor ear heard, neither have entered into the heart of man, the things which God hath prepared for them that love him".

This whole time I am running, trying to be an undesirable soul, unfit for duty of the kingdom, and God is using His people to show me that the love I have for Him is always on display. I felt like I was a walking neon sign at times that says I am running from Christ Jesus. God was showing me that no matter where I was, He was there too. God had chosen me to do a work for Him and He wanted me to be willing to do the things He had purposed.

I was in Fayetteville, NC. I awoke this particular morning with a severe heaviness on me, I felt like an elephant was sitting on and suffocating me. I later learned this is what is called a python spirit. I felt if I didn't make it to church and get prayer through the power of agreement that I was surely going to die. The more God is drawing you the harder the enemy will try to hold on to you and kill you before he sees you go to the Kingdom of Light if possible. I remember driving down I95 at speeds over 85 mph to get to church on time. I had to get my son from his day care first. I made it to prayer three minutes after the appointed time. It was raining outside, and I stood there banging on the door, waiting for the deacon to come to the door and let us in the service. They people were already in prayer and they didn't come. I remember going back to my vehicle and crying, I said "Lord, I don't want to be like this trying to get into heaven. I don't want to make it to the location and have the doors lock me out!" My heart cried out where I had come to in my life. I had truly come to the place where I really wanted to be in the will of God for my life! I wanted to be in the cooperate prayer, I wanted to be in the bible studies, I was craving the presence of God like the scripture says in

Psalms 42:1 "As the hart panteth after the water brooks, so panteth my soul after thee, O God."

I was in a place spiritually, that required the living water, that only God could give me like He told the woman at the well in John 4:13-15. I like her was crying out to God to receive the water that could quench the thirst in my soul. I was eventually let into the service, and I was out of order considering I was wearing pants. I didn't care, I just needed to be in a place to feel God's presence and get prayer.

Little did I know that God was going to give me a visitation and solidify who He had showed me to be in my dreams at the age of fourteen. We were studying the book of Acts 3 there was a man begging for alms at the gate of Beautiful. I will never forget that day because it was a spiritual pivot point. The Holy Spirit gave me a word of knowledge for the congregation on the meaning, of Acts 3:6, I spoke about how Peter transferred his ability to walk in total healing through the anointing of God to the man by faith.

There was another visitor in the church that night, I had never seen him before, after I finished expounding on the Word. The leader of the service asked him if he had anything to add. He stated he didn't but if he could ask me a question. He said "Are you a minister?". I smile, and chuckled, knowing that God had showed me several dreams in my youth and even recently that I was called to minister. I then replied "No, I am not a minister". This minister operated in the Prophetic anointing. After my response, God decided He was going to show up and show not just me but those who were there as well who I was to Him. The minister began to speak about my feelings that day and the press I had done just to make it to the church. He asked me to walk up and down the isle of the church three times praising God, by the time I got to the end of the third turn, I was on my knees, in praise and worshiping God. The heaviness had finally broken. No one in that place know what my struggle was that day. Then like a whirlwind, the presence of God came into the building, it was like a white smoke around the ceiling area in the entire building, and the Voice of God spoke through this prophet these words:

"My child, My Child, you are my chosen, you are my minister, When are you going to tell my people what I have done for you? It is time to be about my Father's business."

Even as I am writing this, I feel the presence of God on me, and I am again moved to tears, because God let me know He had chosen me. Matthew 22:14 tells us : "For many are called, but few are chosen".

I could no longer deny who God had called me to be – His minister. I was to serve God, and His people by spreading the Gospel. I also knew I was called to the nations because I would dream of people that didn't look like me and they were mostly Asian and middle eastern looking in my dreams. I keep this and many other things that God revealed to me to myself because people who were not spiritual would try to discourage what I was knew I called and purposed to do.

Not long after this happened, I started experiencing more divine appointments and connections with people in ministry. One minister who came to that same church, meet me outside as I was leaving from a revival, she had sung so beautifully earlier. Somehow, she asks me what my favorite song was, I told her it was "No ways tired". Her response was "how can a person so young have that as a favorite song?". I used that song as a confession of my faith to strengthen me in the storms that I was in. I was in a place where I felt the only things, I had was my God, my son and a good relationship with my dad. Yes, there was and still are others who love me, but in that season, that was my foundation. That was my anchor. She began to pray with me and during her prayer she asked that God transfer the same anointing on my life to minister, to prophesy and to teach for the glory of God. My life has been filled with moments just like these even to the present. God is continually pouring His spirit out on those who desire to be filled by Him.

Due to a military relocation, I ended up in the mid-west. I knew that this location was a place of transition for me. I knew by going there somethings and people in my life would change. God had revealed that current relationship was over. I had tried to hold on and make it work. However, this person was not in God's will for my life or God's plan. I remember that my prayer life had gotten so strong because of my challenges in my various relationships, work, and other areas. I would go to sleep praying and in my sleep my spirit would be waging warfare. I would wake up speaking in tongues. One night the warfare was so strong that my former lover shook me so hard and yelled that I was speaking in a demonic tongue. The fear of being out of God's will caused me to stop speaking in tongues. I didn't want to be in witchcraft or out of the will of God. This was a tool the enemy used to handicap me from being a threat to his kingdom.

I found a church to be a part of in country I was in at the time. God revealed to the Pastor of that church the call on my life. I wasn't telling no one! I was just trying to live a quiet life. I began to move into walking in the call on my life, and then it seemed as if all Hell broke loose in my life. It got to the point where I made the choice to end my current relationship, that had been over shortly after it began. I was being complacent. I ask to speak to my pastor in the presence of another minister, I didn't want to be accused of trying to get close to the pastor or vice versa. I remember how I felt when I didn't get the support of my leader, after I had made them aware of the physical, verbal, mental abuse and the adultery my then lover was actively engaging. I was told I would never leave him and that I was just being emotional. I know that God had showed me that if I stayed in that situation too much longer, I was going to die either by his hands or his infidelity. That was another pivot point spiritually. I began to speak more to God in prayer and fasting. Then God revealed that what I described was what the 1st Lady was going through in her life. I had called it when I first went to the church. However, the associate I revealed it too made to feel that I wasn't seeing in the spirit realm even though they knew it to be true.

I not only stepped out of ministry, I also left my relationship, left the church and tried to run from my call. Everything except running from my call went well. God allowed me to do like most parents do with their kids. He gave me enough rope to get me to the place where I had to truly decide for Him, I would live or die.

The Transition – Spiritual Awaking

That day was interesting, I had committed a blatant sin, I was bold. I was basking in the thoughts of my sin. As I was driving home, like God always does, He cut the music off, got my full attention and this is what I heard in an audible voice "Who do you think you are that My wrath won't touch you?!!!!". I learned that Grace and mercy does run out. This was a come to Jesus moment for real! Then I heard these words "I will get glory out of your living or your dying the choice is yours!" God reminded me of my free will, but He also reminded me that I was His chosen, therefore He would get Glory from my living or my dying.

That day, I chose to live for God. I repented. I ask God to take the desire for sex away from me until I got married and restore it on my wedding night. I know it was extreme. I had an extreme stronghold of sexual desire in my life. So, I put it the hands of God. Then God called me to a lifestyle of abstinence and celibacy in August of 2012. The walk required getting rid of sex tapes, getting rid of sex toys, getting rid of all the lingerie I had sex with someone previously. I had to really begun living a pure and clean life for God.

I began to really seek God more and more. I even stopped dating because everyone wanted sex. Then God brought women and men of God in my life that were living the same lifestyle. The journey became easier because we were keeping each other encouraged and accountable for our choice to serve God with our body, mind, spirit and soul.

This life of transformation was not just for me, but for the success of my son. I didn't want my son bringing home or marrying a woman who was living the life I was trying to live. As God, worked on my heart and I surrendered areas to Him. There were seasons of stripping the sin from me like peeling layers off an onion for me to reach my spiritual destiny.

It was in this season, that my son was at a very impressionable place In life. God used this process to reach the heart of my son. My greatest success to me is the moment my son chose Christ Jesus as his personal

Lord and savior. God had allowed him to see my process, the hurt, the abuse, the pain, the shame, the healing and the redemption. God used the transformation of my life from sin to ministry as an instrument to impact not just my son's life but others who knew me when I was deep in sin.

It was after I was willing to let go of the things, I had made gods in my life through idolatry that God began to move in my life. He had a minister prophecy to me and told me that He was speeding up the course on my life. I said Lord, what does that mean. I soon learned that I was getting ordained as an Evangelist. One thing about living for God, He has a way of bringing you to the place you should be at a set time. Within a year of my ordination, I was ordained as a Pastor, then I was relocated to Japan in the next few months.

Before my transition to Japan, I went through an Apostolic training ground. When you are obedient to God's instructions you will always be equipped to do what you are called to do. You will also be trained by seasoned saints on how to access the anointing and allow the Holy Spirit to flow without quenching or hindering His Holy Spirit.

This was truly a season of acceleration and redeeming the time of my life where ministry was concerned. It all was the result of a spiritual awaking of seeing how close I was to fulling the scriptures of the wages of Sin is death. It was that day that God did a spiritual renewing in my heart and in my mind that resulted in the developing of the mind of Christ in me. I now seek to experience a continual renewing of my mind. My mindset transition from the things that please my flesh to the things that fulfill the spirit of God in my life.

Now that I entered the season of redemption in my life, a continual process of healing is still taking place. God is always perfecting areas of my life that need healing. I just had to learn to release those areas to Him. A large part of my healing came from the divine connection with my current Apostles.

God will always connect you will the people who operate in the level and gifts of anointing you are to be released into. I tell you, that I got my fire back being connected with this ministry. I remember the day

I got the restoration of my gift of tongues, it happened in the living room of my Apostles home. I desired to have the holy spirit dwell in me with the evidence of speaking in tongues. It happened, now I warfare in tongues daily.

I remember my Apostle pushing me in the spirit and speaking prophetically in my life about what God was planning to do. I desire to serve the Lord, I didn't want to get overly tasked like I had been in my past, and I wanted to enjoy the service.

Little did I know what God had instore for me. I was appointed the Armour Bearer of my Apostle, and that is a fulltime job. I don't mind because everyone doesn't get access to their leader the way that God has given me access. This divine appointment caused me to grow so fast spiritually and to release the dormant gifts inside me to be used for the kingdom of God. The bondage of the spirit of fear has been broken off my life and I am now able to walk not only boldly but deeper in the call God had placed on me.

I remember as part of my training for reigning that my birthday gift was a book called the "Vessel of Honor". Wow, what a powerful book that opened me up to what God had called me to do in the realm of spiritual warfare, there were things that I had dreamed about in my youth that were answered in this book. Notice that God will give you revelation of a thing when you are mature enough to handle the knowledge of the things. My destiny has become one that is greater than I ever imagined and ever thought that I would walk in.

I remember a dream I had as a teenager where I saw a book with the name Dr. T.R. Anderson on it. Well, here we are the book is now a reality. I had to get to the place, where I no longer feared what people would think of me and do what I knew would please God.

This book and my first book have caused many conversations with a couple of elders in my family. I reminded them this is what God has called me to do I must be obedient in doing it. There will be times in your spiritual journey that you will have even those who are closest to you to whisper into your ears to delay the blessings through your obedience.

My obedience to leave the church I was in to go to the place I am now opened the anointing of God for restoration of my gift of prophecy, my gift of Tongues and being able to see into the spiritual realm for the things concerning the heart of God. The Lord is faithful to do the work that He has started in us. I went through some trying of my faith, stretching me outside of my comfort zone, spiritual attacks against my mind and my body, to the place of healing deeply in my emotions.

I no longer respond to the enemies attacks the way I once did, but I wage war in the spirit for the things that are promised to my family, my Pastors, our congregation and the souls of those I have met and will encounter.

I was able to go on my first mission trip to the nation of the Philippines with my Apostle. It was there that God really showed me my passion for the nations. We went to many places on the island every day for a week on our portion of our trip where the children and people had never had medical attention. We took food and medical to them and the Word of God.

It was there I meet so many people who have the same vision for the nations. Divine connections. On the third day of our trip I was given a gift. I didn't open it right away, because I thought it was chocolate. When I did open it, it was an answer to a prayer, I asked God a few days earlier. I asked God what is the total call on my life? I was given a key ring that said, "Prophet to the nations". I was told by the person who gifted it to me that God led them to give me the key ring. Sometimes we don't see ourselves where God has called us because we are not operating in that gift currently. Yet, God will connect you with those who will be spiritual midwives to birth those gifts into your life and ministry.

The connection to my pastors ended with the spiritual promotion in the Kingdom of God to Apostle and Overseer of an International Ministry. That same divine connection pushed me into the greater things God has for me through the birthing of a woman's group called Fearfully & Wonderfully Made that will become a foundation for battered women and single Moms. It also led to the publication of three books, a radio interview, Television interview and podcast interview.

The way God has moved in my life is amazing, but it started with one choice to be live a life of obedience to God. I decided to submit my will to the Will of God and I asked God to align my desires and will to His desire and will for my life. When I did that, I moved from living a mediocre life to a life that is continually growing in blessings in ways I never imagined and the Favor is so great that I am always in a state of continual praise.

God has revealed the hearts of people concerning me! There are some people who will never see me or you beyond their idea of who they feel you should be or how they have labeled and limited you according to their perception of who you are to them. As you walk in the humility and the guidance of the Holy Spirit, some people will see you as God has called you. While others will deny who God has called you to be. Some people will never understand your purpose, the call or the anointing on your life. They will fail to respect the anointing causing them to miss out on blessing that are attached to the anointing on your life.

There is nothing common about what has happened in my life since I made a spiritual decision in the year of 2011 that would catapult me to the place where I am today. I remember this God has given me uncommon faith, favor and blessings!

The way He is moving in my life is nothing common about it and men always want to question what is going on but they can't deny the hand of God on my life. Where God has me now in life and when people question the call on my life it takes me to Acts 10:15 English Standard version "and the voice came to him again a second time, "What God has made clean, do not call common".

As a leader who didn't want to lead because of my understanding and the magnitude of the responsibility attached to the call. I know that the souls were important. I didn't want to fail; fear of failure almost stopped the acceptance of the call.

I thank God for Him having me to push the visions of others. While in that process, before I realized it, I was walking in the call and purpose of my own life. I tried to stay behind the scenes because I didn't fit in, I am peculiar person. People try to tell me that I am not special, I thank God He has shown me who I am in Him. I know that I am not my own as I am now walking boldly in my purpose. I am happy that I stand out for the Kingdom of God and not blending in with what the people think of who I am in the world.

It was through me pushing the visions of others and trying to stay in the place of the follower that God called me to be the leader. God had many impartations of wisdom from the Holy Spirit and those leaders to move me from supporting to the front line of the warfare for the souls of people. God awakened the change agent in me. He has quickened me to use the spear of influence He has given me to impact not only women and men in the United states but also in the Nations throughout the world.

It is my prayer for you, that these pages have opened a doorway for you to walk deeper in your call. That God has given you a greater understanding of how He is able to use each decision you have made to glorify Him in you. You are not too far gone no matter how deep your individual sin, lust and desires are that you are beyond redemption. No one sin is greater than the next it is all equal in the eyes of God! God allowed His son Jesus to die on the cross for the remission of all our sins. If you desire a change, if you feel this is all I can take, enough is enough, I don't and can't live like this anymore, cry out to the God of Abraham, Joshua, Isaac, and allow Him to change your circumstances, renew your mind, heart, spirit and purge your soul and replace your sorrows with the Joy of the Lord which is your strength. I did and now you are seeing the change that God is able to do in you if you allow yourself to be used for His glory, when you surrender your will to the Will of God on your life, the blessings out -weighs the struggles, the joy over cast the sorrows, and the abundance of blessings are never ending as long as you walk in Faith, like a child knowing that your Heavenly Father is there to supply all your needs Philippians 4:19. I declare the peace of God, the wisdom of God be in your life today in Jesus name.

Be blessed as you become who God has called you to be!

www.ingramcontent.com/pod-product-compliance
Lightning Source LLC
Chambersburg PA
CBHW021446070526
44577CB00002B/276